THE
GOSPEL
OF
MARK

GENERAL EDITORS

Gene M. Tucker, *Old Testament*

Charles B. Cousar, *New Testament*

INTERPRETING

I·B·T

BIBLICAL TEXTS

THE
GOSPEL
OF
MARK

Donald H. Juel

ABINGDON PRESS
Nashville

THE GOSPEL OF MARK

Copyright © 1999 by Abingdon Press

This book is printed on elemental-chlorine-free paper.

Library of Congress Cataloging-in-Publication Data

Juel, Donald
    The Gospel of Mark / Donald H. Juel.
      p. cm.—(Interpreting Biblical texts)
    Includes bibliographical references and index.
    ISBN 0-687-00849-2 (alk. paper)
    1. Bible. N.T. Mark—Criticism, interpretation, etc. I. Title. II. Series.
BS2585.2.J83 1999
226.3'06—dc 21   99-28057
                                                     CIP

99 00 01 02 03 04 05 06 07 08—10 9 8 7 6 5 4 3 2 1

MANUFACTURED IN THE UNITED STATES OF AMERICA

For Lynda

CONTENTS

FOREWORD 11

PREFACE 13

INTRODUCTION: INTERPRETING MARK'S
GOSPEL 15

Getting Oriented 15

What Should We Expect? Examining Prejudices 17

What Are We After? Standing and Understanding 21

The Role of the Reader 29

To Teach, to Delight, and to Move: A Rhetorical Approach . . 31

The Three "Characters" in Mark's Gospel 32

What Will We Read as "the Gospel According to Mark"? . . . 43

The Historical Jesus 49

CHAPTER 1
THE OPENING (1:1-15) 53

The Observant Reader and Attentive Listener 54

The Knowledgeable Reader and Listener 57

The Imaginative Reader and Listener 60

Great Expectations 63

CHAPTER 2

THE PLAYERS 65

   Pharisees, Sadducees, and Herodians 66

   Scribes, Chief Priests, and Elders 69

   Satan and Unclean Spirits 70

   Family 71

   Little People 72

   The Disciples 74

CHAPTER 3

WHO IS GOD? 77

   The God of Abraham, Isaac, and Jacob 78

   The God Who Acts 80

   "The Kingdom of God" 81

   God and the Law 82

   God's Future Work 84

   God the Father 85

CHAPTER 4

WHO IS JESUS? 87

   "Who Do People Say That I Am?" Differing Appraisals 88

   "But Who Do You Say That I Am?" A Reader's Evaluation . . 92

   What Language Shall We Borrow? A Brief

      Reflection on Titles 98

CHAPTER 5

PLUNDERING SATAN'S HOUSE 107

   Defeating the Legion (5:1-20) 110

   Freeing Two Women 114

   Where the Devil Did the Devil Go? 117

CHAPTER 6
THE TEACHER 119
"In Parables" 119
Taking Up the Cross: Instructions on Following
   (8:31–10:45) 129
A Glimpse of the Future 132

CHAPTER 7
THE DEATH OF THE KING (14:43–15:47) 139
What Ever Happened to Peter? 141
"As It Has Been Written" 144
"The King of the Jews" 145
The Temple 147
The Way It Is 151
Epilogue: Some Historical Reflections 153

CHAPTER 8
THE DEATH OF JESUS AND THE WILL OF GOD:
A THEOLOGICAL APPRAISAL 157
"The Deep Magic" 160
Beyond the Boundaries 163

CHAPTER 9
ENDINGS AND BEGINNINGS 167
What Shall We Read? 167
Reading the Ending 169
"Those with Ears to Hear" 171
Promises Kept, Promises Not Kept 173

CHAPTER 10
SECRETS AND SECRECY 177
Unseeing Eyes, Unhearing Ears, Hardened Hearts 181
A Test Case: The Disciples 184

    Sight to the Blind 186
    Implied Readers and Actual Readers 189
NOTES 193
BIBLIOGRAPHY 198
INDEX OF ANCIENT AND MODERN AUTHORS ... 199

FOREWORD

Biblical texts create worlds of meaning, and invite readers to enter them. When readers enter such textual worlds, which are often strange and complex, they are confronted with theological claims. With this in mind, the purpose of this series is to help serious readers in their experience of reading and interpreting, to provide guides for their journeys into textual worlds. The controlling perspective is expressed in the operative word of the title—*interpreting*. The primary focus of the series is not so much on the world *behind* the texts or out of which the texts have arisen (though these worlds are not irrelevant) as on the world *created by* the texts in their engagement with readers.

Each volume addresses two questions. First, what are the critical issues of interpretation that have emerged in the recent history of scholarship and to which serious readers of the texts need to be sensitive? Some of the concerns of scholars are interesting and significant but, frankly, peripheral to the interpretative task. Others are more central. How they are addressed influences decisions readers make in the process of interpretation. Thus the authors call attention to these basic issues and indicate their significance for interpretation.

Second, in struggling with particular passages or sections of material, how can readers be kept aware of the larger world created by the text as a whole? How can they both see the forest and examine the individual trees? How can students encountering the story of David and Bathsheba in 2 Samuel 11 read it in light of its context in the larger story, the Deuteronomistic History that includes the books of Deuteronomy through 2 Kings? How can readers of Galatians fit what they learn into the theological coherence and polarities of the larger perspective drawn from all the letters of Paul? Thus each volume provides an overview of the literature as a whole.

The aim of the series is clearly pedagogical. The authors offer their own understanding of the issues and texts, but are more concerned about guiding the reader than engaging in debates with other scholars. The series is meant to serve as a resource, alongside other resources such as commentaries and specialized studies, to aid students in the exciting and often risky venture of interpreting biblical texts.

Gene M. Tucker
General Editor, *Old Testament*

Charles B. Cousar
General Editor, *New Testament*

PREFACE

The challenge of this little volume is pedagogical: I hope to get readers as completely captivated by Mark's Gospel as I have been over the last two and a half decades. It is a mystery to me that some readers still find the earliest of the narratives about Jesus confusing and uninteresting. The reason is not intelligence. Perhaps it is that they have not been properly introduced. Or perhaps it is that they have never heard the words read aloud. I have been blessed with good teachers, and hearing the Gospel of Mark performed was an early and moving experience. My hunch is that readers will view the work differently if they hear the Gospel as well as deal with the printed words and sentences. I would heartily recommend that anyone taking the trouble to read this book invest time reading Mark's Gospel through several times, preferably aloud. It will also prove beneficial to do that reading in concert with others.

Having time to write requires support. I am grateful to Princeton Seminary for a sabbatical leave and to the Center of Theological Inquiry for providing a splendid place to work. My colleagues at the center were stimulating conversation partners, among whom I would single out for special thanks Dr. Mark Reasoner for his helpful comments and questions—and his willingness to drop everything and look over a draft or listen to an idea. I am regularly impressed by how much I have learned in teaching Mark with my colleague Patrick Keifert for a decade and a half. Most of all, I am grateful to a generation of students, many of whose names I have forgotten, whose little observations and discoveries have immeasurably enriched my own reading.

PREFACE

Special thanks are due my assistant, Elisabeth Johnson, for her careful attention to the manuscript and preparation of the index.

The last word of gratitude must be for my wife, Lynda, whose love and support over the years mean more than I can say.

INTRODUCTION

INTERPRETING MARK'S GOSPEL

GETTING ORIENTED

Crucial to interpretation is knowing where to begin. Bible reading, of course, has no prerequisites. Anyone can pick up a Bible and start reading. It may be argued, in fact, that anxiety about being fully prepared to interpret the Bible can actually inhibit reading and enjoyment. This volume is written with confidence that there is nevertheless much to learn that can enhance our understanding and appreciation of the Bible.

An important stage in the development of educated readers is learning how much has been written about the Bible. With an almost limitless amount of information available on the text of the New Testament, the history of its translation and interpretation, the historical and cultural context out of which it emerged, and the ways it is currently read by experts of all sorts, a student needs to recognize what is important to know. It is impossible to read everything, even for those who study full-time. Further, gathering information does not necessarily result in enlightenment. Information may contribute little to making sense of the Gospel, or it may result in making sense of something uninteresting and unimportant.

As important as knowing *where* to begin is knowing *how* to begin. It has been customary within academic circles to begin engagement with the Gospels in silent, solitary reading. In classes where students can work in original languages, the initial assignment may be to translate the first chapter. This will take a good bit of time for most students and will offer an experience of a particular sort. The exercise will offer a glimpse of only a small portion of the Gospel and is thus more likely to focus on details. Those who know the language at all will immediately recognize Mark's limited vocabulary and rather elementary constructions. They may notice the repetition of simple connecting links ("and immediately") and the episodic character of the narrative. They may be taken by the strangeness of a story told in a language other than their own, captivated perhaps by individual details ("Why this word?"). And they are easily impressed by scholarly arguments that point up the aesthetic shortcomings of the Gospel.

Another initial assignment is to work with a synopsis of the Gospels—an arrangement of Matthew, Mark, and Luke in parallel columns—and to read the opening sections of Mark in comparison to the sections in Matthew or Luke. Such reading calls attention to the very different ways of beginning a story, as well as differences in detail and vocabulary. Some commentaries proceed this way, noting regularly that "while Mark says this, Matthew or Luke say something different." The approach makes clear how differently the same story can be told and how dramatically the differences shape the reader's expectations and experience of the narrative.

More recently I have sent students off from their first class to read Mark from beginning to end in translation (in their own language; the presence of students who do not speak English and whose Bible is in another tongue makes for interesting comparisons from the outset). Their observations and questions are different. They are less likely to be taken by particular words than by scenes or themes or the whole story. Often someone will ask why Jesus silences people he heals; someone else, a more careful reader, will ask also about the exception, where a former demoniac is instructed to go and tell. A retired schoolteacher commented, "I was impressed with the number of imperatives. Jesus is always commanding someone or something." Some will note parallels or duplicate forms of a story, like the feeding of the five thousand and the four thousand. They are less likely to be impressed by arguments that point out the aesthetic shortcomings of the narrative.

When students begin by watching a "performance" of the Gospel by one of several accomplished readers, sometimes live but usually videotaped, they react very differently. Few, if any, are impressed by the alleged literary flaws of the Gospel. It "works" orally. And people are more likely to react emotionally—to laugh, to become irritated, or to experience uneasiness. Deciding that 16:8 is the best choice among alternative endings after a lengthy discussion of what is involved in choosing among various possibilities present within manuscript tradition has an impact nothing like that of a two-hour performance of Mark that ends with, "And they said nothing to anyone, for they were afraid." Students are more taken by Jesus' tone of voice, or the elusive roles of characters who appear and disappear.

Finally, when students are asked to study the Gospel in preparation for reading themselves, aloud in the presence of others, another whole series of questions arises that never occur to those who read silently and privately. It matters a great deal if the Bible is interpreted to understand its meaning or if it is read with an eye to actually performing it. Knowing where to begin and what will be relevant to study depend upon the goal of the engagement with the Gospel. How we choose to study, in other words, depends upon what we imagine the Bible is good for.

WHAT SHOULD WE EXPECT?
EXAMINING PREJUDICES

Few people come to the Bible without some expectations. Preparation may be subtle. That the New Testament is read in schools and in churches—and has been read for almost two thousand years—suggests that the various writings are valuable. Those who find the writings like Mark strange or difficult are at least encouraged to press on, knowing that others have found them meaningful. Preparation is also more overt. Churches have always introduced people to the Bible. In the Middle Ages, cathedral windows depicting biblical stories provided the lenses through which people looked at the Gospels. Church music, from hymns to oratorios, combined passages from a variety of biblical works and gave to the biblical text a particular feel or mood. For the more scholarly and literate, there are collected opinions about who wrote the Gospels.

People who know anything about church tradition—or who read the paragraphs introducing each biblical book that appear in study Bibles—will have learned that according to an old tradition, the "Gospel according to Mark" was written by a follower of Peter and onetime traveling companion of the apostle Paul, perhaps a Jerusalem believer in whose house the church met (Acts 12). It comes as a surprise to many that the Gospel itself says no such thing. It is utterly mute on the matter of authorship and occasion. We will spend a little time reviewing the history of interpreting Mark, not so as to feel superior to previous generations of readers but to understand where we stand, how our expectations have been shaped, what suggestions will or will not stand up to critical scrutiny, and what hunches are worth following up.

The first person to say anything about the book we know as the Gospel according to Mark is a bishop named Papias, who lived in the early decades of the second century in Hierapolis in Asia Minor, some of whose words have been preserved by the great fourth-century church historian Eusebius. According to Eusebius, this is what Papias "used to say":

> Mark was the interpreter of Peter. He wrote down accurately, but without form *[ou mentoi taxei]* what he remembered of the things said and done by the Lord. For neither did he hear the Lord, nor did he follow him, but later on, as I said, Peter—who fashioned the teachings according to the needs of the moment, but not as though he were drawing up a connected account of the Lord's sayings. Thus Mark made no mistake in so recording some things as he remembered them. For he had one thing in mind, namely to omit nothing of the things he had heard and to falsify nothing among them.[1]

With so little information about Papias and the context in which he writes, scholars have disagreed about how to understand his comments. Those scholars interested in Mark as a possible historical resource for getting back to the real Jesus of history tend to think that Papias was interested in the "order" of Mark's story: "Mark wrote down accurately, but not in order [i.e., chronological], " since disagreements among the Gospel writers about the exact sequence of events in Jesus' ministry pose a problem for historians trying to get at what really happened. More recently, interpreters interested in literary and rhetorical questions have tended to read Papias's words as a comment on the literary form of Mark: Mark wrote accurately, but without the form or "order" one expects of written works.[2] Mark's Gospel, in other words, does not sound like proper literature. I tend to agree with this reading of Papias's comments.

In either case, the first recorded comment on the work that we know as the Gospel according to Mark reflects some embarrassment about it and a need to offer an apology. Mark did what he was supposed to do, says Papias. His goals were modest. He recorded what he heard from his source (Peter), who also had no literary pretensions. His only concern as an author was to be complete and accurate. One ought not therefore expect too much of the work.

The good bishop's sense that Mark is a strange book is reflected in the entire history of the church. Mark's Gospel is virtually ignored. Matthew, then John, are the Gospels that were most widely read and quoted.

A more important reason for the lack of attention paid Mark's Gospel is the work of another bishop, the influential Augustine of Hippo, who lived and worked in the early fifth century. Somewhat embarrassed by the presence of four Gospels instead of one, Augustine sought to give some reason for the abundance. Mark, he argued, was the "epitomizer" of Matthew. That is, Mark abridged Matthew's Gospel. His arguments make some sense, since almost everything in Mark's Gospel can be found in Matthew—except that Matthew includes other material as well (e.g., the Sermon on the Mount, birth stories, accounts of the Resurrection). The relationship of Mark to the other Gospels is an important matter and will occupy us later. If it is true that Mark is only a shortened version of Matthew, it is not surprising that church leaders and teachers preferred the "real thing" (Matthew) and ignored Mark.

That Mark is a secondary version of Matthew was held almost without question into the nineteenth century. Griesbach, the

German scholar perhaps most responsible for the use of a synopsis of the three "synoptic Gospels" as a study tool (an arrangement of Matthew, Mark, and Luke in parallel columns), was convinced that Matthew wrote first, Luke next, and Mark later ("Matthean priority"). His synopsis, however, provided one of the tools by which students of the New Testament began to look more carefully at the relationship among Matthew, Mark, and Luke, eventually concluding that Mark was most likely the first Gospel narrative to be written. A nineteenth-century scholar named Karl Lachmann is credited with arguing in a convincing way that Mark was the earliest of the Gospels.

The arguments for "Markan priority," as it is known, have convinced most scholars. The patterns of shared wording among Matthew, Mark, and Luke seem to demand a literary solution—that is, one or more of the Gospel writers must have seen the work of the other(s) or all have a common source. Scholars have found it easier to explain Matthew and Luke as expanded rewrites of Mark than the reverse. Augustine's argument that Mark abridges Matthew, for example, cannot explain why in some of the miracle stories Mark's version is far longer and Matthew's sounds like a condensation (e.g., Mark 5:1-20 and Matt 8:28-34). The Greek of Matthew and Luke is in general superior to Mark's and in specific instances can be viewed as conscious improvement. The greatest difference between Matthew and Luke, on the one hand, and Mark on the other, is the considerable body of Jesus' sayings common to Matthew and Luke that are absent in Mark. The standard explanation is that there existed a collection of Jesus' sayings (called "Q," for *Quelle*, the German word for "source") shared by Matthew and Luke. In addition to the two common sources—Mark and "Q"—Matthew and Luke apparently had independent sources as well. The matters are well discussed in standard introductions to the New Testament.

"Markan priority" provided a considerable boost in the popularity of what now came to be known as the earliest Gospel. Ironically, what attracted scholars to Mark in the eighteenth and nineteenth centuries was the same alleged lack of artfulness signaled by Papias centuries earlier. These scholars were principally interested in the Gospels as historical resources. Some were convinced that Christian writings had distorted the facts of history, making an ordinary Jew into the Second Person of the

Trinity. A whole variety of scholars took their turn in writing about the "real Jesus" in hopes of rescuing Jesus from the rigid doctrines and tired piety of the church. Mark was important to them as the earliest available source for their reconstructive project. The alleged artlessness, coupled with the remarkable sense of verisimilitude, seemed to make the Gospel invaluable as a source. The author, according to this view, simply collected material but was (fortunately) too unsophisticated to transform it into a coherent narrative. Matthew and Luke, being more creative, were more likely to have altered traditions to make them fit into their literary productions. Well into the twentieth century, a prominent German scholar could say of all the Gospels that their authors were not really "authors" but "collectors, vehicles of tradition, editors."[3]

One great exception to this whole tradition of scholarship was Wilhelm Wrede, whose book on the so-called Messianic Secret, published in 1901, treated Mark's Gospel as a creative piece with a theological agenda.[4] While not claiming too much for the Gospel writer's literary or theological sophistication, Wrede nonetheless appreciated Mark's achievement, which was to produce a new genre of literature. He did this, Wrede argued, by combining the tradition about Jesus that did not view him as Messiah with the tradition that proclaimed Jesus as the crucified and risen Christ, most clearly articulated in Paul's letters (e.g., 1 Cor 15:3-7). Had scholarship found Wrede's work more persuasive, it might have come to focus on the Gospel narrative rather than its sources. That was not to be. Not until the 1950s would a major shift in scholarship occur that would direct attention more to the narrative than to what lay behind it.

WHAT ARE WE AFTER? STANDING AND UNDERSTANDING

Sorting out alternative strategies for reading is itself an interesting topic and can become all-absorbing. We could spend all our time thinking about how to proceed, only to discover that we have no time to read the Bible. That would be unfortunate. A few moments of reflection will prove useful, however. I would like to suggest spatial images by which to understand what we are after and what sorts of questions will prove most helpful. The images—the "World Behind the Text," the "World of the Text," and the "World in Front of the Text"—are borrowed principally from the philosopher Paul Ricoeur. They are both simple and useful in locating ourselves among the various traditions and methods of interpretation.

The World Behind Mark's Gospel: Interpretation Through Dissection

Students of Mark in the nineteenth and most of the twentieth century have been interested in the Gospel principally as a window that affords a glimpse of an earlier period in the history of tradition. As interpreters, our task is to stand before the window and look through it at the various things it allows us to view, which may include the actual recorded events, the "intention" of Jesus or the church or the Gospel writer.[5] Questions have to do mostly with how reliable a window the story provides. Is the glass tinted, or does it distort? The elaborate methods that allow such an assessment all begin with source criticism, that is, trying to break the story down into its various sources. If the narrative were a seamless cloth, source criticism would be far more difficult. The episodic nature of the Gospel, however—whole series of anecdotes with abrupt transition from one to the next—can be studied as evidence for the book's compositional history.

That such dissection of Mark can be done with such ease is indeed impressive. In a famous study,[6] the German Karl Ludwig Schmidt demonstrated that when a handful of summaries are removed from the narrative, the story disintegrates into individual episodes or collections of episodes. The author, he argued, has provided a primitive framework within which to set bits and pieces of prior tradition, like a mosaic. Because Mark's technique is so undeveloped, it is relatively easy to show how the whole was fashioned. If the Gospel can be compared to a mosaic, one may study the Gospel by observing the use of individual stones. One result of this observation has been *form criticism,* a school of interpretation that focuses on the form of individual story units as an indication of their function.

The school of *form criticism* took as its point of departure the features of written biblical works that seem to betray the marks of oral culture. Borrowing insights from studies of folklore in

German and Scandinavian universities, students first of the Old Testament, then of the New Testament, undertook the task of reconstructing the communities who told stories about Jesus and remembered his sayings. Typical of the oral setting in traditional communities are features that make for easy remembering or that facilitate performance. Most easily recognizable are confessions and hymns and liturgical texts that can be isolated in Paul's letters. Paul's summary of "the gospel which I received," for example, has a simple structure that scholars identify as "confessional" (1 Cor 15:3-7). Jesus' words to his disciples at the Last Supper that Paul recalls in 1 Corinthians 11 seem to betray the marks of regular usage in a worship setting (1 Cor 11:23-25). While formal patterns are not so clearly identifiable in narrative material, form critics were convinced that they could identify "controversy stories" and "miracle stories" and "wisdom sayings" for which a regular setting in the life of the community could be identified.

An example of this kind of formal analysis is the case of what some call "controversy stories." In the second and third chapters of Mark's Gospel, Jesus engages in discussion with Pharisees who question his practice:

> And as he sat at dinner in Levi's house, many tax collectors and sinners were also sitting with Jesus and his disciples—for there were many who followed him. When the scribes of the Pharisees saw that he was eating with sinners and tax collectors, they said to his disciples, "Why does he eat with tax collectors and sinners?" When Jesus heard this, he said to them, "Those who are well have no need of a physician, but those who are sick; I have come to call not the righteous but sinners." (2:15-17)

> One sabbath he was going through the grainfields; and as they made their way his disciples began to pluck heads of grain. The Pharisees said to him, "Look, why are they doing what is not lawful on the sabbath?" And he said to them, "Have you never read what David did when he and his companions were hungry and in need of food? He entered the house of God, when Abiathar was high priest, and ate the bread of the Presence, which it is not lawful for any but the priests to eat, and he gave some to his companions." Then he said to them, "The sabbath was made for humankind, and not humankind for the sabbath; so the Son of Man is lord even of the sabbath." (2:23-28)

The anecdotes include regular features. There is a general setting, a question is posed—usually in form of a challenge or criticism—and Jesus gives a short, pointed response. Those unfamiliar with Jewish ritual matters will have some difficulty following the discussions. We will have occasion to deal with that issue later. Here we should notice the simple formal patterns in which the episodes are cast.

Such patterns can be studied and compared with other story forms. In the recorded writings of the Jewish rabbis, for example, controversies about legal matters are a regular feature of interpretation. The forms are somewhat different. Answers to questions are often structured according to two responses, one from the "house of Shammai," and one from the "house of Hillel" (two prominent first-century rabbis). An opinion is given, sometimes with the argument, followed by an indication that this is the view of the majority. Often a minority opinion is recorded. Such forms are similar to other legal discourse. This is the way lawyers and judges talk—and the way they remember cases. The form of the story reflects something about its function in a regular social setting.

Students of the Bible have argued there also exists such a relationship between New Testament "forms" and a regular social setting they reflect. Controversy stories seem to imply a community that was interested in matters of sabbath observance and purity laws that settled such matters not by gathering the opinions of respected teachers but by recalling sayings of Jesus.

What scholars hope to learn from such study is something about the setting in which the material was remembered and used. Who were the anonymous people who handed on stories about Jesus and remembered them? What were their interests? Interpretation is understood here as providing the materials with which to reconstruct a history of the early church—or at least to reconstruct the "original" audience of the various traditions that have found their way into the written Gospels. The focus of interpretation is the practices and beliefs that characterized this particular group of people—thus, their "mind." To read the Gospel of Mark is to have insight into the lives of real people in the first century of our era.

"Controversy stories" suggest a group invested in questions having to do with Jewish legal observance. Whether or not the issues in the stories arose from actual controversies in Jesus' ministry, the questions make sense within the later setting of the church. Why are we casual with regard to sabbath observance? What about fasting? Should we not be more careful about food laws? The criticisms aimed at Jesus identify a matter still important to the faithful. The answers to the questions in the form of pithy sayings of Jesus indicate how the community understands itself and its practices, and they suggest one of the ways in which Jesus serves as an authority.

For such study, the narrative is dissected into its components, whether these are cycles of stories or individual episodes. Such analysis of sources does not yield "history" in the sense of getting back to events in the ministry of Jesus, but history as an earlier stage of tradition, most likely oral and not written. While these traditions can be studied to determine their historical reliability, they can also be examined for what they disclose about the people who remembered such stories and handed them on.

Such dissecting of the narrative can move in two directions. On the one hand, those interested in the "historical Jesus"—the Jesus who can be reconstructed through critical use of sources, including the Gospels—can continue to work behind the alleged oral sources from which Mark drew. Such scholars formulate criteria on the basis of which to test the historical reliability of these oral sources (see below on the historical Jesus). On the other hand, the same information can be examined for what it discloses about the author of the Gospel. If we know Mark's sources, we can study the way he combined them to form the present Gospel. Many scholars are convinced, for example, that Mark was the first to write a whole story of Jesus and that his sources were at best cycles of stories and perhaps a small collection of parables, as well as a longer and more coherent account of Jesus' trial and death. How he chose to tie them together to tell a story is partly revealed in how he does his editing or redacting (thus *redaction criticism*). The focus of interest here is the peculiar views of the author, understood as somehow distinct from those of the tradition that he edited, and thus most visible in overt changes or alterations of sources.

Both form and redaction criticism, as the approaches came to be called, study the Gospel by taking it apart. The disciplines take seriously the form of the story units and the cultural setting in which they developed. They take less seriously the final form of the narrative. Like Papias, they tend to find it aesthetically lacking. The interest of such scholars is not first of all in the narrative as a whole, which they do not find coherent or compelling, but in the personalities it discloses or the historical facts it reveals. That the Gospel is a coherent piece that intends to be performed is something they ignore or reject.

Scholarship in the last twenty-five years has made a decisive break with such approaches, not because the methods of study are invalid but because interpreters choose to focus on a reading of the whole narrative or an experience of it. Dissecting a narrative to make sense of it turns out to be more like an autopsy than an operation. The doctor may learn many interesting things by carving up a human body, but something must die as a result. We will be interested principally in the Gospel as a story that comes to life when read.

The World of Mark's Gospel: Literary Analysis and Gospel Narratives

A crucial shift in scholarship occurred in the midfifties. Scholars trained in source and form criticism whose strategies were to dissect the narratives so as more closely to study the component parts suddenly became interested in the body. Willi Marxsen's *Mark the Evangelist* was one of the first to use the methods of source criticism to speak about the "evangelist" and to ask after the message of the whole.[7]

Methods derived from an earlier era were soon supplemented by approaches more common in the field of literature. The chair of the English department at Indiana University published essays on Mark.[8] Major literary scholars like Frank Kermode began publishing studies of Mark and other Gospels.[9] Within the guild of New Testament scholars, a major force in refocusing scholarship was Norman Perrin, who turned his considerable energies to study the evangelist rather than the historical Jesus. His *What Is Redaction Criticism?* marks an important transition from an era dominated by source criticism to a new era in which literary study in the proper sense began to flourish. While he speaks of redaction criticism, Perrin means something quite different, more akin to the kind of study familiar from literature classes.

The fundamental premise of redaction criticism, then, is that the pericope can be analyzed from the perspective of a Marcan purpose. The goal of such analysis is to understand the purpose and the theology that is revealed in the purpose. To this end we concern ourselves both with the individual parts of the narrative and with the story as a whole. In other words, we analyze the constituent parts of the narrative ... to see what they tell us of Mark as one who gathers, modifies, or creates tradition, and we analyze the total narrative in terms of its overall purposes ... to see what this will tell us about Mark as an evangelist.[10]

For those who were not trained as source critics, it may be difficult to imagine the impact of the shift. A generation of Bible readers had been trained not to read stories, and their training was successful. Those who read Mark with historical interests never imagined the book worked as a story. Fine scholars never observed the simplest connections within the story that students pick up almost immediately—provided they look for such things. In the story of Jesus' trial, for example, Peter's denial of Jesus "brackets" the actual trial report. The narrator takes Peter as far as the courtyard of the high priest (14:53-54) before shifting to the proceedings inside (14:55-65), only to shift back to Peter when Jesus' trial is over (14:66-72). The breaks in the story turn out to be more than signs of deficient sources. The shifting from the outside to the inside and back is a simple way of relating the two episodes. Once that becomes apparent, all sorts of things stand out. Perhaps the most obvious is the relationship between the taunt of those pummeling Jesus at the conclusion of his trial ("Prophesy!" [14:65]) and the events in the courtyard (14:66-72). The narrator informs us that after Peter's third denial, the cock crows—for a second time. The detail is important because Jesus predicted that "before the cock crows twice, you will deny me three times" (14:72). Careful readers will recall that prophecy (14:28-30). One of Jesus' prophecies is being fulfilled to the letter—at the moment Jesus is being mocked as a prophet inside the house. Readers are expected to appreciate the irony in a way no one in the story can. The relationship between the mockery and Peter's denial seems obvious—but not a single commentator preoccupied with Mark's sources ever noted it.[11] Seek, and you will find.

Scholars now speak of Mark's "bracketing" or "intercalating" the account of Jesus' trial (14:55-65) with the story of Peter's denial (14:54, 66-72) as a feature of style and not simply a mark of connected sources. The bracketing of the cleansing of the Temple with the cursing of the fig tree works in similar fashion (11:12-26). Once the stylistic feature is identified, patterns begin to appear throughout the narrative. It may be, for example, that the whole story of Jesus' ministry is "bracketed" by the *tearing* of the heavens at Jesus' baptism (1:10) and the *tearing* of the Temple curtain at his death (15:38).

The host of works on Mark that have appeared in the last twenty years have assumed that the Gospel is a whole fabric to be appreciated. Robert Tannehill published a significant essay on the disciples in Mark, asking about their "narrative role."[12] The theme of discipleship has been treated systematically in the work of Ernest Best.[13] The trial and death of Jesus became a particular focus of study.[14] David Rhoads and his colleague in the English department at Carthage College, Donald Michie, wrote a literary study of Mark,[15] nicely complemented by Rhoads's performance of Mark's Gospel (at first live, then recorded on video). Mary Ann Tolbert[16] and John Donahue[17] have read Mark, taking the parables in chapter four as a point of departure.

What is crucial here is not the particular literary methodology chosen or the concept of narrative. The point is more basic. One can read Mark's Gospel as a whole story. Individual pieces are important as they relate to the other parts of the whole. If Mark's Gospel is like a mosaic, one needs to stand far enough away to glimpse the whole picture.

The World in Front of Mark's Gospel

Books are not the same as pictures. While the analogy may be helpful, Mark's Gospel is not a mosaic or a weaving. It is a story that intends to be read. While silent "readers" can dissect the words or even appreciate the whole construct of words and sentences, Mark's Gospel was written to be heard, and hearing requires performance. Attending plays or symphonies is a more apt analogy. Crucial is what happens at the present moment, when the work comes to life. Experiencing a performance is not the same as studying. There is less distance. That is all the more apparent when we are called upon to perform and not just to listen. Analyzing Mark's Gospel should include reflection on what happens "on this side of the text" as well as what is "in" the story or "behind" it.

THE ROLE OF THE READER

A school of interpretation has developed that studies literature by focusing attention on the reader. It is for readers (or hearers), after all, that books are written. What they "mean" is at least as much a function of what readers get as what authors intend. This approach, associated with scholars like Stanley Fish, questions whether it is really helpful to speak about "texts" at all, given how much depends upon reception and how differently books can be read by different audiences.[18]

In a monumental work entitled *Let the Reader Understand*, Robert Fowler has helped New Testament studies focus on the role of the reader in the enterprise of reading and interpreting. While virtually all scholarly energies have been focused on the author and the "author's intention," Fowler demonstrated how literature actually works with an audience.

> Literary critics have until recently given slight attention to the reader and the reading experience. To cite one glaring example, Robert Scholes and Robert Kellogg, in *The Nature of Narrative*, describe narrative as "distinguished by two characteristics: the presence of a story and a storyteller...For writing to be narrative no more and no less than a teller and a tale are required." Someone to hear the story or, in the case of literature, someone to read it was apparently too obvious to mention. Yet why tell a story if no one is there to listen to it? Who writes a story not expecting it to be read?[19]

Seeking to remedy the deficiency, he focuses his attention on the audience of Mark's Gospel—or perhaps more accurately, on the interplay between the narrative and the readership. His work provides an important transition to a more rhetorical approach. His argument is that literature "works" by shaping the experience of an audience. Features of the narrative are not important in themselves but are part of an interaction involving an author and an audience. While we may speak of "intention," it cannot exclude the desire to move an audience, and any such interaction requires attention to the experience of reading as well as writing.

Right
Fowler

His discussion of irony is particularly helpful. Irony is not a property of narrative, as though it existed in and of itself. "Irony" is the effect on a reader. Following Seymour Chatman, Fowler distinguishes between story and discourse. The story (or "text") is the material itself; "discourse" is how it impacts a particular hearer, on our side of the printed page. Irony works by awakening in the reader a sense of distance from the narrative audience. It becomes clear that the reader hears words as meaning something different from what they mean to characters in the story. As readers, we can understand why the Roman soldiers might think the claim that Jesus is "King of the Jews" worthy of sport (15:16-20). Jesus looks nothing like a king. Dressing him in royal garb and kneeling in mock homage gives them an opportunity to demonstrate the distance that separates pretenders from real power, serving also as a reminder to others of what happens in the real world to those who oppose Caesar. At the same time it is clear to readers that the soldiers are saying more than they know. Their words are true in a way only readers can appreciate, who know that Jesus is the Christ, the Son of God (see below). Distinguishing the material (story) from the way it affects the reader (discourse) is necessary to appreciate what occurs when the story is heard by a real audience.

This emphasis on the reader requires attention to "the world in front of the text"—the realm in which the words on the page take life as they are read and appreciated. It may be useful to speak of what is "behind" Mark's Gospel, since there was a history that led to its writing. It is useful to speak of the "world" of the text in the sense that pieces are part of a larger whole that has a structure and themes and order. Books are written, however, to be read and heard. Interpretation ought to attend first of all to the event of reading, not least because words intend to move an audience as well as to inform. It is on this side of the Gospel we stand, after all, among contemporaries in whose company we read. Summarizing the "point" of a parable in a sentence or two is hardly the same as appreciating what happens when a parable is read to a particular audience. Our strategies of reading and interpretation ought to have as their goal a richer and more sensitive reading and hearing of the Gospel of Mark. To that end I wish to suggest an approach that may be called "rhetorical."

TO TEACH, TO DELIGHT, AND TO MOVE: A RHETORICAL APPROACH

There has been a burst of activity in recent years that falls under the general heading of "Rhetorical Criticism." The strategy arises from an appreciation of the persuasive character of all speech—in particular, the speech-literature of antiquity. The case is perhaps most obvious for Paul, who wrote letters to particular congregations to move them in a variety of ways. Letter writing was something learned in the schools that trained people for public life. Letters were a substitute for personal presence, but even in the absence of the writer, the letters were read aloud by someone. The rules for writing and speaking are thus not as far apart as they might be for us. When the purpose of the letter is to persuade, the "rules" of rhetoric generally apply.

The Gospels are no less persuasive literature. The author of Luke-Acts says explicitly that he is writing "in order that you may recognize the certainty of the things you have been taught" (Luke 1:4, my translation); the author of the Fourth Gospel writes so "that you may believe that Jesus is the Christ, the Son of God, and that believing you may have life in his name" (John 20:30-31 RSV). While the agenda is not stated as explicitly in Mark, we may presume the narrative is written to move an audience. Interpretation that focuses on the rhetorical will want to know more about the desired persuasion and the strategies adopted. "Strategies" here does not necessarily imply conscious reflection or calculation on the part of an author but an appreciation of how an author actually seeks to make a case and to convince.

Traditional biblical scholarship has usually attended to such matters by asking historical questions: Who was the author of Mark's Gospel? What can be known about the original audience and their location? Many within the discipline of biblical studies have understood themselves to be historians, interested in the Bible as something that, to be understood properly, must be located at another time and place for a distant audience. A prominent New Testament scholar put it this way: "The task of the biblical scholar is to understand what the original author intended for the original audience."

One might propose, on the contrary, that the task of biblical scholars is to help a contemporary audience understand the

Bible, and that the task of a contemporary audience is to experience the force of the narrative's argument in the present. Historical information may be important for such an enterprise, but it is neither the beginning nor the end of the task. Some biblical scholarship has become an exclusively historical discipline, interested in the Bible as an artifact of the past. That will not be the strategy pursued here. The "rhetorical approach" we will take focuses on the contemporary setting of the Gospel, on "this side of the page."

The task of the interpreter is different if the image used of engagement is drawn from the aesthetic world of drama and music. The student of Euripides' plays will read them differently if the goal is a production at a local theater, whether one participates as director, actor, or audience. Many things will go into such a production, including learning as much as possible about Greek theater and its rules. Of interest, however, is what happens when the narrative comes to life. The language plays here, on us and our contemporaries. The question is, How can we be both faithful and effective in our performance of the play and perceptive and receptive as an audience? Interpretation that stops short of actual engagement and performance is akin to reducing a great play or symphony to a few sentences about its "meaning."

How does Mark's Gospel "work" with an audience? The question need never be asked until it comes time to read. Why are there so few transitions? One may offer explanations of the episodic nature of the Markan narrative based on a hypothesis about sources and how the Gospel was written. But for performers and audiences, more interesting is how the episodes will "play." Do the individual episodes put off an audience, or do they engage readers? The impressiveness of oral presentations suggests the Gospel is effective in such a medium. A rhetorical approach may focus on how it teaches, delights, and moves.

THE THREE "CHARACTERS" IN MARK'S GOSPEL

One of the things a rhetorical approach highlights is the relationship among three "characters" in any act of communication. There is the character of the speaker, the character of the speech, and the character of the audience. Interpretation that does not reflect on all three will yield an inadequate account of how literature and speech work. Aristotle's three categories have proved helpful for centuries. They may provide a good place to reflect on the sorts of things that should interest us as we read and interpret.

Who Is Telling the Story?

It is normal in our culture to study a work by asking about the author. We like to know about writers—who they are, when they have lived, how they feel about things. An effective way to market a book is to arrange appearances for the author on talk shows. Perhaps the most important thing to say about the author of Mark's Gospel is that he (presumably a he) chooses to remain anonymous. At no point are we given a direct glimpse of the author, as in the opening verses of Luke's Gospel (Luke 1:1-4). And while the "author" is not necessarily identified with the narrator, in Mark not even the narrator intrudes with an "I heard" or "I saw" or "I think." The only author we can know—apart from the one created by church tradition—is the one "implied" in the Gospel narrative. That author chooses to remain in the shadows or offstage, and the narrative strategy he employs allows no place for evaluating the work in terms of our personal knowledge of the writer—despite the endless curiosity about the "historical" Mark.

This has implications for interpretation. It is quite common to speak of the intentions of an author. Where something is unclear, it would be most helpful to ask the writer, "What did you mean by this?" We have, of course, no such access to the biblical writers. Not only are they long dead, but they are not in any explicit sense available to us. We may learn a few things about Paul from his letters. We know the Gospel writers only through the story they tell and how they choose to tell it. Those interpreters who try to correlate features of the Gospel with the ideas or feelings of "Mark" are engaged in fiction. The creation of the "historical Mark," the alleged author of the Gospel who was a disciple of Peter, is interesting for what it discloses about interpreters throughout history. That "historical Mark," however, is not terribly useful for actual engagement with the Gospel narrative. Few convincing arguments can be made about the particular identity of the author; even less convincing are attempts to read the mind of this hypothetical historical figure.

What we know from reading the Gospel is a narrator. In modern literature narrators can be reliable or unreliable. In the Gospels, the narrators are reliable. That is surely the impression we are given in Mark. The impersonal narrator is never corrected. Judgments about characters turn out to be true. The opening identification of Jesus as "Christ, Son of God," is confirmed by God, who calls Jesus "Son" on two occasions (at Jesus' baptism [1:11] and at the Transfiguration [9:7]). Other supernatural beings—unclean spirits—likewise confirm that Jesus is "Son of God" and "Son of the Most High God." With the name Judas Iscariot, the list of the disciples includes the comment that he was the one "who betrayed him" (3:19). Later in the story we are told how Judas goes to the Temple authorities to betray Jesus (14:10-11). We have every reason to believe the insights we are given ("they were jealous"; "they were utterly afraid"). Summaries are particularly important in gathering together themes and focusing them (1:32-34; 3:11). In miracle stories we depend on the narrator for appreciating the plight of the ones who come to Jesus for help (5:3-5, 25-26).

The narrator is not limited, as are the characters in the story. His perspective is far more encompassing and penetrating. Perhaps this is what the church has meant by "inspiration." Mark's Gospel does not make explicit claims for itself, but its mode of narration implies an extraordinary claim to authority.

The character of the narrator will be a major feature in constructing the author, whom we call "Mark." That narrator must be given voice in order to come to life, however. If we ask about who is telling the story, the fact is that in public, some particular person is doing the telling for the ancient narrator. How should the narrator be embodied in a reader/performer? Should the reader be a baritone or a tenor, a mezzo or a coloratura? There are no stage directions. Anyone can read. How they embody the narrative, how they give it voice, will differ. Significant differences may require some adjudication. Who is correct? The legitimacy of a performance must take into account the effect of a particular reading as well as the "meaning." What does hearing the passage do to readers? What should it do? Does it instill confidence in the narrator among readers? Does it raise anxieties or challenge long-held conventions? While such questions are more difficult than simple historical or literary queries, they will make for a far more lively and interesting engagement with Mark's Gospel.

Readings disclose the character of the reader. A student attended a performance of Mark's Gospel by a famous actor. During the performance she became uncomfortably aware that she was coming to view the performer as an unbeliever. She had no idea about the actor's personal faith; all she knew was the impression he was giving through his reading. The particular occasion was his portrayal of the disciples as buffoons. His performance elicited no sympathy and offered no hope of their eventual redemption. In her view, that disposition toward the disciples conveyed the impression of someone who had no investment in the story and no sense of its future. The performer might have been surprised by the reaction. He might have indicated it was not at all what he intended. Embodying the story nevertheless has such effects on an audience—and may even reveal an "intention" the performer does not recognize in himself or herself.

Attention to the character of the "implied author" can serve as discipline for our own reading and hearing. That we have no access to the historical author of Mark's Gospel does not mean we are completely at a loss about the author. There are important things we learn about the "implied" author—the sum total of judgments behind the story that we may reconstruct—for whom the narrator presumably speaks:

1. The work is written from the perspective of a believer. From the outset we know that the story is the "good news of Jesus Christ" (1:1). While the story is told anonymously, it is told from the perspective of someone invested in the story.
2. The work is written in simple Greek—not translation Greek, as one might expect of an author whose native language was other than Greek (e.g., Aramaic). The author available to us is not "literate" in the sense of following aesthetic convention and does not expect readers to find that a fatal flaw. Mark's Greek is the ordinary language of the street—not typical of literature of his day, where literature was produced by the upper classes largely for upper-class enjoyment.
3. The author knows the scriptures of Israel (the Christian Old Testament)—in Greek. The scriptures are quoted on some occasions, alluded to on others, and perhaps echoed else-

where. The author apparently expects readers to know the scriptures. The second line, "As it is written in the prophet Isaiah," presumes that readers know who Isaiah is and will be impressed that Jesus' story has something to do with Isaiah's prophecy.

4. The author is familiar with Jewish customs and beliefs. The religious community is divided into Pharisees, Sadducees, and Herodians; at other times, into scribes, chief priests, and elders. Among the Gospel writers, this author is the most careful to distinguish various groups within the larger Jewish community. Jesus is questioned about ritual matters like sabbath observance and purity regulations. Apart from one explanation (7:3-5), the author presumes readers understand what is at issue. Even in the extended discussion of ritual purity in chapter 7, which explains what "the Pharisees, and all the Jews" do, the narrator explains Pharisaic purity rituals in technical terms, presuming familiarity with terminology and issues among readers.

Forming an impression of the "character of the speaker" is an important aspect of interpretation. Our task must also include forming an impression of the audience.

Who Is Listening to the Story?

One way to approach the question of audience is to ask the historical question: Who were the people for whom the work was originally written? As in the case of the author, we are once again on unstable ground. There are no sure markers of the particular occasion and location of composition. One of the crucial events used to date the Gospels is the destruction of the Temple in Jerusalem by the Romans in 70 CE. Do the various Gospels give evidence that they were written after this crucial event? The question is complex, first of all because none of the authors purports to trace the story of Jesus' followers to this date. Even Acts ends the story about a decade before the Temple fell. Evidence, therefore, will be indirect. Mark was most likely written after the destruction of the Temple. That serious scholars can still argue for a date prior to 70 indicates just how insubstantial the evidence for dating is.

 The same is true for locating the composition geographically.

Tradition locates Peter in Rome where he was apparently martyred. If "Mark" was a companion of Peter, it is possible that his Gospel was written in Rome. Lacking convincing evidence about the identity of the author and his relationship to Peter, however, the composition can be located almost anywhere Greek was spoken—which, since the time of Alexander the Great, was virtually the whole Mediterranean world. The attempts to locate the composition of Mark in Syria or Rome again indicate a lack of hard evidence.[20]

Another way to address the question is to begin an actual audience's experience of reading. How are readers to be involved in the story? Readers are addressed directly only two times, both in chapter 13. The first address is an allusion to Daniel: "When you see the desolating sacrilege set up where it ought not to be (let the reader understand) . . . " (13:14, alluding to Dan 9:27). The second comes at the end of Jesus' address to a small group of his disciples: "What I say to you I say to all: Keep awake" (13:37). Readers are "present" at other obvious points, as when the narrator gives translations of Aramaic phrases Jesus uses (5:41; 7:34; 14:36; 15:22; 15:34). This became obvious as a student "performed" the story of Jesus' raising of Jairus's daughter. To make the story dramatic, the student looked down at an imaginary little girl and said, "Talitha cum." Without looking up, he added, "which means, 'little girl, get up.'" It was immediately clear to the audience that the comment was not for the little girl but for readers who would not understand Jesus' words.

Elsewhere, readers stand apart from the story, benefiting from the narrator's commentary on what is occurring as well as access to events (like the "confessions" of the demons) to which participants in the story are apparently not privy. *maybe*

Some argue that the "task" of readers is to identify with characters in the story. That seems a limited notion of engagement. First, the Gospel story does not paint characters as "typical," with the exception of those Jesus heals who are rarely named. His disciples are given names. Jesus is not at all typical. He is identified from the outset as singular: "the Christ, the Son of God." Demons testify to his special character: he is the Holy One of God, the Son of God, and the Son of the Most High. The passion narrative does not depict Jesus as an exemplary sufferer or martyr but as the mocked and crucified "King of the Jews," "the Christ, the Son of the Blessed One," and "the Christ, the King of Israel," "God's Son." It would seem more likely that the narrative makes it almost impossible for readers to identify with characters in the story. As readers, we are cast in the role of insiders, privy to information we share with the narrator and not the players in the story.

In determining our role as audience, we are once again limited by our historical distance from the story. Yet, as with the author, we can learn about the people for whom the work was written—the "implied audience"—by asking what they are expected to know. While the glimpse of "audience" is limited, the exercise is worth the effort: it may offer to present-day readers a sense of where study is necessary simply to recognize some basic knowledge the author presumes for the audience (like knowledge of the Old Testament). We may note the following:

1. Readers are expected to know a great deal: about geography (where is the Jordan, Capernaum, Tyre and Sidon, the Decapolis, Bethany, not to mention Jerusalem?), about people (John the Baptist, Herod, Caiaphas, and Pilate, about whom little is said), about the scriptures and their interpretation (see esp. Mark 12), Jewish rituals (sabbath observance, dietary matters, and purity requirements), about specific terminology ("the Holy One of God," "Son of God," "Son of the Most High God," "the Christ"). Both the content of the story and the lack of explanations presume readers with knowledge and particular interests. It is significant, for example, that the author expects readers to be concerned about sabbath observance and that Jesus "declared all foods clean" (7:17-19).

2. Readers do not think of themselves as "Christians." The term never appears in the Gospel. There are a few indicators that readers include Gentiles, most notably the extended explanation of washing practices in chapter 7, but there are at least as many that the majority of readers are Jews—most likely Jews, however, who belonged to the "Jesus Movement." We must be careful, therefore, about characterizing the readers of the Gospel in terms of their relationship to Israel.

3. Readers speak Greek and read (or hear) Israel's scriptures in Greek (the Septuagint).

Readers are not merely taken as they are, however. Any story "constructs" a reader, placing him or her in a particular position and making all sorts of demands. We shall have occasion to return to this feature of the story, but at least a few preliminary observations may be made:

1. Readers must exercise their imaginations if they are to make sense of the story. In the opening scenes, few explicit connections are made. Readers know that John the Baptizer is speaking about Jesus in 1:8—not because John or the narrator says so, but because Jesus is mentioned in 1:1, and because immediately after John's promise about the "stronger one" who will come after him, Jesus appears on the scene.
2. Readers are cast in the role of insiders from the beginning of the Gospel. "Identifying" with any characters in the story is made difficult when we hear what no one else can and receive explanations unavailable to those in the story. The impersonal narrator invites readers to watch the story unfold from a privileged position as people who are told from the outset that the story is "the good news of Jesus Christ, the Son of God" (1:1). As hard as we may try to sympathize with the disciples, we know what they cannot. In the account of Jesus' trial and death, readers are in a position to appreciate the irony of what is occurring as Jesus is invested and acclaimed as "King of the Jews" by people who have no idea that what they are saying is true. If there is some "secret" about Jesus' identity in the story, readers of the story are related to that secret differently from the characters.

Precisely how are readers to relate to the story? Historical questions about an ancient audience are important and helpful; at least as relevant are observations that have to do with actual readers in the present. Perhaps the question is best deferred until an actual engagement with the narrative. Certainly those who perform the Gospel relate to the narrative very differently from those who silently evaluate its meaning and reliability. One of our tasks will be to determine what would count as a reason for reading (and responding) in a particular way. And that cannot be determined in advance. There is no such thing as a universal audience. Appreciation of the story depends on single hearers. Individual experience is not the end, however. Reading and interpretation are public matters. Personal experience of the Gospel should contribute to a conversation in which it may be critiqued and enriched, so that the community of readers is built up and the hearing and reading of the Gospel become richer. My own reading of Mark is an extraordinary mosaic composed of little insights provided by a host of students. I do not imagine my hearing of the Gospel is any more completed now than it was some decades ago when I began my studies.

What Are We Reading?

If we are to view the Bible as literature, we must recognize its distinctive features. Those accustomed to psychological novels devoted to an exploration of character will recognize the Bible as something different. As for Aristotle, plot is perhaps the most important feature of Mark's narrative. Characters are largely flat. We are given little insight into the psychological profile of any of the characters, even Jesus. We are introduced to him without any glimpse of the forces that brought him to be baptized by John. What was his family life like? Who were the influential people that shaped his decisions? And the disciples—Why were Peter and Andrew, James and John willing to leave their occupations and families to follow? What about the disciples who are only named? What did they think? Why did Judas betray Jesus? The story is uninterested in such questions. The reason may be that the author does not know the answers. More likely, it signals that the story is about other things, social and political realities rather than psychological. Jesus is important as one who changes the face of the world. Crucial in interactions with others is not how he feels but how they respond—not just at the moment, but over the course of the story. Why is it that Jesus must die? Why does he so unsettle and alienate the religious and political leaders that they decide to do away with him? What will their rejection and Jesus' death have to do with his message about the kingdom of God? How will God respond?

Do we have reason to believe such questions are worth asking? As we have noted earlier, many readers have come to Mark with low expectations. Common among scholars from the very first comments about Mark is an uneasiness with its literary form. No less a scholar than Albert Schweitzer could speak of the Gospel as "inherently unintelligible."[21] The dramatic shift in appreciating the earliest of the Gospels in the last twenty-five years requires some sort of explanation.

Making a case for the aesthetic shortcomings of the Gospel has not been difficult. The episodic character of the story, the lack of transitions, lack of motivation for characters are all visible. Equally impressive is how well the narrative works when it is performed. It may be, of course, that the coherence experienced by an audience is due more to the work of the performer than the work—but the mere fact that the Gospel works in an oral setting shifts the discussion.

The presence of "doublettes" is a good example. In Mark, there are two accounts of Jesus' miraculous feeding of people in the desert. In one, he feeds five thousand (6:35-44); in the other, he feeds four thousand (8:1-9). Scholars have tended to view the two stories from the perspective of the tradition "behind" Mark's Gospel and to see them as two versions of the same story. In this view, Mark is too unsophisticated to appreciate the duplication. When the stories are performed, however, the experience is most interesting. When Jesus tells his disciples to feed the crowd in the second account (8:1-3), they seem utterly bewildered: "How can one feed these people with bread here in the desert?" (8:4). Jesus' question, "How many loaves do you have?" (8:5) may be played with a touch of sarcasm and weariness. In the performance of Mark by David Rhoads, audiences actually laugh at this point, at the disciples' expense. This experience of the second feeding story is possible only because a few moments earlier (in terms of narrative performance) the same scene has been enacted: the disciples panic, Jesus takes the few loaves they have and miraculously feeds the thousands. The disciples have apparently learned nothing. Whatever conclusions one may draw about sources, the two stories play off one another well in their present context. How to evaluate them depends entirely on what interpreters deem as important.[22]

Another reason for the increased appreciation of Mark is an awareness of—and even preference for—alternative narrative strategies. Modern readers have a particular sense of what it means to say a story is "realistic." A story that moves smoothly, without mystery and ambiguity, tying up loose ends, may strike readers as having little to do with the world they know. The context in which the story is read is, as we have noted, an important factor in appreciating the Gospel.[23]

In the following chapters we will examine the major players in the story, with a particular focus on the various aspects of Jesus' ministry. We will examine major themes and read closely some important passages. The goal is not to be comprehensive but to suggest ways of approaching the Gospel that will deal with its various features. The strategy emphasizes performance of the Gospel for contemporary audiences, since that is what books are for. While we may speak of historical matters, the Bible intends to shape the imagination of each new generation of readers who will find promise in its pages.

Over the last few decades, engagement with Mark's Gospel has proved to be stimulating and evocative. Mark's Gospel has suddenly become perhaps the most popular. No single reading has come to dominate the world of scholarship and the church, perhaps one reason for its popularity. A rhetorical strategy should be less concerned with arriving at the one correct interpretation than with making possible actual engagement with a story. Only when the narrative comes alive among real audiences can we speak about what it means and how it seeks to move us. The more inclusive the audience, the richer the hearings.

Study is significant. There are things to learn about the language of the Gospel and the world of which it is a part. The story makes particular claims about Israel's God and specific individuals, notably a Galilean Jew named Jesus who lived at the time of Pontius Pilate. Reading Mark's Gospel will involve appreciating its particularity and taking such claims seriously. Greater familiarity with the story, its characteristics and plot, will likewise enhance appreciation. Study ought not make unnecessary a reading of the Gospel, but should facilitate a richer experience for those who read and hear. While there are other strategies that may be valid, I will emphasize those that hold the most promise for enhancing engagement with the story. The analogy to the study of other works of art and music is instructive: we study Shakespeare's plays and Beethoven's symphonies so that the next time we hear them performed we will be a more appreciative audience and the works will come to life in new ways. The same should be true of our study of the Bible.

WHAT WILL WE READ AS "THE GOSPEL ACCORDING TO MARK"?

Before beginning our reading of Mark's Gospel, we ought to spend a few moments thinking about the actual book we will be using. There are several alternatives, and educated readers should know what is involved in deciding among them.

The Text

It may not be obvious to those studying "the Gospel according to Mark" that they must decide which "Gospel of Mark" to read. Those whose Bible has been the Authorized Version of 1611, prepared by translators appointed by King James, will discover that "Mark" in the RSV, NRSV, NIV, NEB, or TLB is different from the one they have known. Sometimes the differences are insignificant. On other occasions they are weighty. King James's Mark reads as the second verse, "As it is written in the prophets, 'Behold...'" (1:2); modern translations read, "As it is written in Isaiah the prophet." In 15:28, the KJV reads, "And the scripture was fulfilled, which saith, And he was numbered with the transgressors"; in modern translations there is no 15:28. A footnote at the end of 15:27 reads, "Other ancient authorities add verse 28." Most important, in the KJV, Mark's Gospel continues through verse 20 in chapter 16; in modern translations, Mark's Gospel ends with 16:8 (usually followed by a complex set of footnotes and alternative endings). What people know and experience as "Mark's Gospel" depends entirely on what translation is used.

In the three instances above, the difference between the KJV and all modern translations is that the king's translators had a different Greek text from which to translate. The NT writings were written in Greek, not the language of Jesus but of the next generation of believers. Prior to the invention of the printing press, works were written by hand (manu-scripts) on papyrus paper or animal skins, on scrolls or in book form (codex). Since the Bible became an important book, it was copied—by hand—many times. As a result of the work of archaeologists and collectors of ancient libraries, we now have access to thousands of handwritten copies of the Bible or portions of it. All extant manuscripts of the New Testament are from codices and not scrolls.

Not surprisingly, there are differences among the handwritten manuscripts. Some are small variations in spelling; others have to do with whole lines of text. Because there are so many copies of NT works, someone must decide what will be printed. The problem is quite familiar to students of literature, who must prepare "critical editions" of novels or dramas that have come down to us in multiple editions. We would prefer to have a play of Shakespeare as he wrote it—and not as it has been "improved" by copyists. Deciding on what is "original" is a complex business, however. Students working with several editions of the same text must develop some principles on the basis of which to decide among alternatives. This enterprise, known as textual criticism, is of particular significance for students of the Bible. Scholars have no access to original authors, nor to original editions of any biblical work. They must sort through all known copies, compare the texts, identify differences, and choose among them. They must do so for the simple reason that publishers must have a single text to publish.

The history of the NT text is a fascinating one. Looking at the manuscripts that have been located and deciphered—sometimes only with the help of modern X-ray or photographic techniques—one can only be impressed by the whole enterprise. Behind all modern translations lies a Greek text that has been constructed by text critics from known evidence. Differences among manuscripts have been evaluated, and finally committees have had to vote on what choice to make. Sometimes the choices are relatively easy; on other occasions complete agreement is impossible given conflicting evidence. In any case, "the Gospel according to Mark" to which we have access is translated from a critical edition that is the creation of scholars and still subject to change. The most important reason for using a modern translation rather than the King James Version is that the Greek manuscripts on the basis of which the king's translators did their work were no older than the tenth century. Today, we have manuscripts from the fourth century and fragments from much earlier times.

The differences with which we began—in 1:2, 15:28, and 16:1-8—all depend on decisions made among alternatives. When a group of manuscripts reads "written in the prophets" and another reads "Isaiah the prophet," a text critic must ask which is the more reasonable original reading. Number of manuscripts and their age are relevant but not as important as other factors. Crucial here is an understanding of copyists who transcribed the text. Is it likely that a copyist has changed a correct ascription to an incorrect—or is it more likely that a scribe has "improved" what appears to be an error? The citation in Mark 1:2 is not only from Isaiah, in fact, but also from Malachi, which makes it likely that a scribe has sought to correct the text by changing it to "the prophets." The most reasonable text, therefore, is the more difficult.

While 15:28 is present in a large number of manuscripts, it is absent from a group that has proved to be the most reliable. Is it more likely that a scribe has added the "proof from the scriptures" or omitted it? Relevant here is the way scriptural material is handled elsewhere in the passion story. Scholars reckon that it is easier to explain the addition of the verse from a pious scribe than an omission. Scribes tend to expand texts rather than abridge; thus the principle "the shorter text is generally to be preferred." Verse 15:28 therefore belongs not in the "Gospel according to Mark" that will be printed but in a footnote indicating what "other ancient authorities include."

The ending of the Gospel is a particularly interesting—and significant—textual problem. We will examine the matter in detail later in the volume. At this point it may be enough to note that on the basis of the two standard principles by which the work of scribes is analyzed (the more difficult and the shorter readings are generally to be preferred), 16:8 should be regarded as the most likely among all the alternative endings the manuscripts offer.

The "Gospel according to Mark" to which we refer, therefore, is the product of scholarly committees who continue to sift available evidence and rethink the arguments for and against particular choices. The latest "critical edition" of Mark, used by the vast majority of scholarly readers, is the twenty-seventh edition of the Nestle-Aland Greek New Testament. A twenty-eighth edition, with some changes, will be forthcoming. Modern readers of the Bible owe an enormous debt of gratitude not only to the anonymous scribes who painstakingly copied biblical works but also to the textual critics who painstakingly sorted through available manuscript evidence to produce the only "Gospel according to Mark" to which we have access.

TRANSLATING THE TEXT

Very few people read the Bible in its original languages. Someone, therefore, must assume responsibility for taking the critical edition of the Greek text of Mark and rendering it in ordinary languages people use. The amazing variety of translations indicates there is more than one way to translate. Those who are unable to read Hebrew and Greek should probably consult a variety of translations to get a sense of the possibilities. Readers should know something about the theory behind the particular translation they favor. Introductions to the various Bible translations are often very helpful in making such matters clear.

Translators must make various sorts of decisions. One is how to "voice" the Gospel. The language of the King James Version sounds like Shakespeare, probably because it is the language of the great master of drama from the early decades of seventeenth-century England. That may suggest to contemporary English-speaking readers that Mark should sound like a classic, using a vocabulary that presumes two years of college education. The Greek of Mark is quite different, however. The story is not cast in the language of high literature. Mark's Greek is the language of the street, with a simple vocabulary and sometimes primitive syntax. A comparable language in our contemporary setting would undoubtedly strike people as too colloquial for church.

Decisions by translators shape the experience of reading. In Mark, Jesus regularly uses an unprecedented Greek phrase as a self-reference, variously translated "the Son of Man," "the son of Man," "the human one," or "the Man from heaven." Knowing how to render the phrase is made difficult because the particular expression does not occur outside the Gospels. The use of capital letters (the Son of Man) suggests that the expression is a title, while "the son of man" may point in a different direction. Without more knowledge, readers of the English text will believe what they see. Most modern translation committees regard "the Son of Man" as a title with some implied content.[24] A growing number of scholars doubt that is the case. Because the original Greek manuscripts are written throughout in capital letters, we cannot rely on them for clues to our own practice. Those who must rely on English translations will in such cases benefit from comparing English versions.

In Mark 1:10, the RSV reads: "And when he came up out of the

46

water, immediately he saw the heavens opened." The NRSV reads, "And just as he was coming up out of the water, he saw the heavens torn apart.... " Neither quite captures the sense of the Greek term *schizomenous*, which suggests an ongoing action ("being torn apart"). The NRSV is far closer to the sense of the Greek word, however. It is difficult to imagine how a translator could render the verb *schizo* as "open"—except that Matthew and Luke both use the same Greek verb, different from Mark's, which is best translated "open." The translation in the RSV probably reflects the ancient tendency of reading Mark through the eyes of Matthew.

One of the differences between "opened" and "torn" is the impact of the term. Though there is a core meaning both share, one term ("opened") suggests something natural, perhaps even peaceful; the second ("torn") is a far more violent image, perhaps dangerous. Another result of the translation in the NRSV is that readers who know only English may discover a relationship between the initial image in Jesus' ministry ("the heavens were being torn apart") and the concluding image ("the curtain of the temple was torn in two" [15:38]). The same Greek verb is employed in both passages, the only two occurrences in the whole Gospel. Their relationship is obvious and suggestive, as we shall see. Without sensitive translating, however, English readers cannot appreciate the parallel and a whole dimension of potential meaning is lost.

The NRSV will be cited regularly throughout this work, except in places where an alternative translation seems required. Those who have no access to the Greek are dependent upon translators. While that may have an unsettling effect on serious students of the New Testament, it is an important reminder that reading the Gospel according to Mark is a cross-cultural exercise. There are differences among languages and language systems, as those who have studied a language other than their own are aware. Not recognizing the differences is to risk captivity to a kind of imperialism that assumes everyone thinks as we do and experiences the world as we do. Awareness that translations are interpretations and that serious readers should consult more than one is a mark of humility proper to those who seek to engage the Scriptures. It likewise serves as a reminder that we owe a debt of gratitude to those translators who struggle to make the Bible accessible to people in every language under the heavens.

VOICING THE TEXT

Biblical literature was written to be heard. The majority of people in the New Testament world could not read.[25] Their access to literature was through an oral medium. Even those who read for themselves made sounds when they read. The sound of the words is an aspect of their reality that many never experience in our contemporary culture that has developed a very different view of language.

Because the Gospel of Mark is still part of an oral culture in contemporary churches, the question about bringing the text to life orally remains an issue. It may even be the case that people who read to themselves supply a voice. The question is what the voice sounds like. Most "performances" of the Gospel in churches are uninspired. People have even been taught not to inflect their voices lest they interpret the sacred text. The result has been boring readings. There are alternatives.

Those who have watched the performance of Mark by someone like Alec McGowan or David Rhoads understand how different the same words can be made to sound. Actual speakers can, of course, accomplish a great deal by body language and gestures. Even simple alterations in voice can make a difference, however. One particularly dramatic example is in determining how to "play" the role of Pilate in Mark's story of the passion. A prominent feature of the story is Pilate's interchange with the crowds.

> So the crowd came and began to ask Pilate to do for them according to his custom. Then he answered them, "Do you want me to release for you the King of the Jews?" For he realized that it was out of jealousy that the chief priests had handed him over. But the chief priests stirred up the crowd to have him release Barabbas for them instead. Pilate spoke to them again, "Then what do you wish me to do with the man you call the King of the Jews?" They shouted back, "Crucify him!" Pilate asked them, "Why, what evil has he done?" But they shouted all the more, "Crucify him!" (15:8-14)

When Pilate addresses the crowd, is he sincere or mocking? "What shall I do with the one you call the King of the Jews?" Perhaps he is asking a sincere question. Or perhaps it is a taunt. "The one *you call*" can be ironic; Jesus is on trial as king only because the Jewish leaders have brought him to Pilate. They have said it all. The point is explicitly made in the Fourth Gospel, where the priests ask Pilate to change what he has written from "This is the King of the Jews" to "He said he was the King of the Jews." "I have written what I have written," says Pilate (played with a wry smile) (John 19:21-22). Perhaps Pilate's exchange with the priests and the crowd is a taunt from the Roman official who is enjoying the irony that his subjects have turned on one of their own at Passover when they are commemorating deliverance from bondage to Pharaoh. That they are requesting the aid of Caesar's governor in disposing of their "King" is too good an opportunity to pass up. If this is how we are to experience the story, reading the verses in public will require a note of sarcasm in Pilate's voice. Such a tone will surely change dramatically the way people experience the story. The additional irony that Pilate is speaking the truth indicates how rich the passage is and how much thought can be invested in determining how it is to be played.

A refusal to make such decisions and to take responsibility for voicing the text in a particular way is itself a decision about how to bring the words to life—or more accurately, how not to bring them to life. Readings are always embodied. How to think about the particular embodiment is an important aspect of biblical interpretation, even if it has not been a regular feature of biblical scholarship.

THE HISTORICAL JESUS

The strategy I am commending is one that understands the narrative as a whole and respects its ability as language to move and to shape imagination. The story is important not simply because it has "meaning" but because it has power.

"But is it true?" The question will be asked no matter how prominently literary and rhetorical questions are highlighted. When they ask, people usually mean, "Did that really happen? Was there someone named Jesus? Was he baptized by John in the Jordan River? Did he cast out demons? Was he crucified under Pontius Pilate? Was he raised from the dead?" While often betraying a limited notion of language that understands words primarily as pointers to something more "real," outside language, the questions also reflect a proper appreciation of the Gospel story. It is particular. The parables—the figurative language—are clearly marked: "the Kingdom of God is like...." The rest of the narrative refers to particular people and places and times. Such narrative may still be fictional, but it at least demands a different sort of evaluation. Mark's Gospel makes claims about a specific historical figure named Jesus. Its truthfulness, if not exhausted by questions of historical reliability, surely includes them.

Here clarity is important. Even raising historical questions suggests there are reasons for doubt. Some faithful Bible readers refuse to grant the legitimacy of doubt. They understand the truthfulness of the scriptures to be a matter of faith. That is to misunderstand the nature of "historical argument." Historical studies are a realm of human intellectual endeavor. Claims to truthfulness within the historical realm must be made according to rules of argument and use of evidence. Without good reasons, the assertion that Mark's Gospel is historically reliable is only an assertion, and the "game" of historical inquiry operates according to good reasons. Pronouncements of the faithful may be personally satisfying, but they do not change the community of inquiry. They do not convince the neighbor. Christians have engaged in historical study with their neighbors because they have recognized the legitimacy of the questions and the need to test convictions.

The rules for historical argument are not peculiar to faith traditions. They are worked out within a community of inquiry. What we expect of historical deliberation is not certainty but probability. "True" in this case has to do with what reasonable people can be expected to give their assent to after a case has been argued.

It matters what case is being argued. The group known as the Jesus Seminar has stirred up controversy by publishing its own version of the Gospels, offering an appraisal of the reliability of Jesus' sayings. The most certain are in red, probable in pink, improbable in gray, and highly unlikely in black. People must understand what the published volume intends. The seminar has asked itself the question, "About which of Jesus' sayings can we offer a convincing argument?" Their criteria are stringent because they want to identify an "assured minimum," excluding material about which anyone might have a doubt. The volume suggests there are few of Jesus' sayings we can prove he said beyond a doubt, given available evidence and rules of historical argument. That is hardly surprising.

The study might be done differently. Someone might publish a volume that asks which sayings we can prove Jesus did not say. The results would be the reverse: virtually every passage would be in red, since there is always the possibility that Jesus said or did such a thing even if we cannot prove it. The volume might appeal to troubled believers but would hold little interest for the general public. The interesting historical arguments will be in the pink and gray areas. What might be said historically about the Jesus tradition with some degree of confidence?

This volume is not a contribution to the study of the historical Jesus. There are many fine volumes devoted to the topic, with Albert Schweitzer's *The Quest of the Historical Jesus* perhaps the most important, though written nearly a century ago. This study is devoted to a reading of Mark's Gospel that will enhance the ability of the work to delight and to move. Nevertheless, because the Gospel makes historical claims, students of Mark can be expected to take historical questions seriously—and they may thus expect the same of this volume. I tend to find the work of the Jesus Seminar less convincing than the work of other less "radical" scholars. I think it quite possible to sketch a profile of Jesus from the Gospel accounts that credibly locates him in a particular historical environment. My personal opinions, however, are less important than arguments. I have included a discussion of the reliability of Mark's narrative in the chapter on the death of Jesus, since this is the central feature of the story. The discussion will necessarily include reflection on how we make historical arguments and what should be convincing. For the moment, it is to the literary and rhetorical tasks that we turn.

CHAPTER 1

THE OPENING (1:1-15)

The beginning of the good news of Jesus Christ, the Son of God. As it is written in the prophet Isaiah,

"See, I am sending my messenger ahead of you,
　who will prepare your way;
the voice of one crying out in the wilderness:
　'Prepare the way of the Lord,
　make his paths straight.'"

John the baptizer appeared in the wilderness, proclaiming a baptism of repentance for the forgiveness of sins. And people from the whole Judean countryside and all the people of Jerusalem were going out to him, and were baptized by him in the river Jordan, confessing their sins. Now John was clothed with camel's hair, with a leather belt around his waist, and he ate locusts and wild honey. He proclaimed, "The one who is more powerful than I is coming after me; I am not worthy to stoop down and untie the thong of his sandals. I have baptized you with water; but he will baptize you with the Holy Spirit."

In those days Jesus came from Nazareth of Galilee and was baptized by John in the Jordan. And just as he was coming up out of the water, he saw the heavens torn apart and the Spirit descending like a dove on him. And a voice came from heaven, "You are my Son, the Beloved; with you I am well pleased."

And the Spirit immediately drove him out into the wilderness. He was in the wilderness forty days, tempted by Satan; and he was with the wild beasts; and the angels waited on him.

Now after John was arrested, Jesus came to Galilee, proclaiming the good news of God, and saying, "The time is fulfilled, and the kingdom of God has come near; repent, and believe in the good news."

THE OBSERVANT READER
AND ATTENTIVE LISTENER

Contrary to the kinds of expectations generated by academic institutions, one does not need to know anything to appreciate Mark's Gospel. Much of what is necessary to appreciate the story is available to observant readers and careful listeners.

For example, the story begins with an assessment: what follows is "the beginning of the good news of Jesus Christ, the Son of God." The story is good news; in what way, we are not told. What is meant by the "beginning" is likewise left unexplained. Already readers may begin to form an agenda of questions to ask as the story unfolds.

What follows is a reference to something "written in the prophet Isaiah..." Even without knowledge of the Old Testament, readers have a sense that the "beginning" is somehow related to some ancient promises.

The speaker of the words is not identified, as in Luke. When read silently, the reader may imagine a narrator (and behind the narrator an unidentified author) whose character and personality emerge as the story is told. When read aloud, the lack of a specified author forces the reader to make a decision whether to serve as advocate or, conscious of the possibility, to make the audience aware that he or she is at least ambivalent about what is being said and thus has a critical relationship with the "inscribed narrator." Those who listen are from the outset placed in the position of insiders who learn what characters in the story cannot know.

The first character we meet is John the baptizer. We learn that he is enormously popular, that he is a fire and brimstone preacher, and that his diet and clothing are unusual. None of these things is explained further. His diet and clothing apparently mark him as peculiar. Some knowledge of the geographical setting (especially the proximity to Jerusalem) and the peculiar clothing adds depth to the story but is not necessary to appreciate what is happening.

While John proclaims "a baptism of repentance for the forgiveness of sins" (1:4), his only recorded words have to do with a successor:

> He proclaimed, "The one who is more powerful than I is coming after me; I am not worthy to stoop down and untie the thong of his sandals. I have baptized you with water; but he will baptize you with the Holy Spirit." (1:7-8)

His words, the first to be spoken by a character in the story, serve as a prophecy—interestingly, a prophecy that is not immediately fulfilled: "He will baptize you with the Holy Spirit" (1:8). Those who read carefully will come to the end of Mark's story without having learned about Jesus' having baptized anyone with the Spirit. When asked about this, students generally point to Acts as the place where the promise is fulfilled. Mark writes no sequel to his Gospel, however, and particularly if Mark is the earliest of the Gospel stories, the absence of a narrative like Acts 2 is all the more interesting. This is the first in a series of promises that are not fulfilled by the time the story ends. What to make of them will be important for interpreters.

Jesus is introduced virtually without preparation. We have been offered an assessment: he is Christ, Son of God (1:1). But the particulars of his background—his birth, education, credentials—are completely omitted. We learn only that he comes to be baptized by John. Even for those who know virtually nothing about the terms "Christ" and "Son of God," that Jesus—presumably the protagonist in the story—comes to be baptized for the forgiveness of sins will seem peculiar. There is no effort to explain the tension, in contrast to Matthew's account in which the dialogue between John and Jesus at least acknowledges the problem (Matt 3:14-15).

The account of Jesus' baptism is as interesting for what it does not say as for what it does. Peculiar is the failure to mention anything about John's view of things. We have no idea if the Baptizer recognizes who has come to be baptized, no sense that he appreciates what has occurred. The reactions of others present are likewise not mentioned, perhaps because they are unimportant. Most striking is the failure to say anything about Jesus' reaction. We learn nothing about his own feelings. While people in our society are interested in little else, the story is not played out at the level of the psychological. How Jesus feels, what motivates him, what has influenced him to decide as he does—these are apparently unimportant compared with the public consequences of his arrival. Readers are expected to be more aware of the political and social dimensions of life than the psychological.

The spectacle of the heavens being torn open, the Spirit descending on Jesus, and a voice from heaven making a declaration about "my Son" contrast with the public reaction: there is none. The narrator says only that "he (Jesus) saw"; the voice addresses him: "You are my Son." Is this perhaps a vision? There are no clues that it is. It is described in the same matter-of-fact style as the rest of the narrative. It is difficult to imagine what a "tear in the heavens" might look like and even more difficult to imagine that no one but Jesus noticed. We can only wonder that the narrator and reader hear what only Jesus appears to see and hear. Readers and listeners are cast in the role of "insiders."

Once again, to appreciate the story readers do not need to know what it means that Jesus is called "my beloved Son" by the voice from the torn heavens, or that someone is "pleased" with him. It is enough to recognize that the events are singular. We are not given to imagine that such features accompany other baptisms. Jesus is obviously special—as we have been told.

What it means that the Spirit comes down "on" Jesus (NRSV) will become apparent as the story unfolds. The immediate consequence is that Jesus is "driven" into the wilderness where he is "tempted" by Satan. Without knowing more, readers can assume this will be important for future tests Jesus must face.

Finally, the coordination of the beginning of Jesus' public preaching and John's arrest foreshadows another sense in which John will be a "forerunner."

THE KNOWLEDGEABLE READER AND LISTENER

Those with access to a Bible with footnotes may learn a most interesting thing about the opening verses: versions of Mark in ancient manuscripts do not agree. Some important manuscripts lack "Son of God" in the opening line; experts on the text of the New Testament agree that deciding on which version to print and which to relegate to the footnotes is difficult. Some ancient versions read "as it is written in the prophets" rather than "in the prophet Isaiah," a reading followed by the old King James Version. Verse 4 occurs in four different versions among the manuscripts, and the passage chosen by textual critics features a grammatical infelicity not preserved in the English translation.[1] Even deciding what will be read as "the Bible" requires decisions among alternatives, as we have noted earlier.

While much is available on the surface of the text, the narrative takes on texture and richness when readers know some particulars. The citation of a passage from Isaiah, for example, links the story of Jesus to a whole set of images from Israel's scriptures and tradition. The prophet Isaiah in turn writes within a rich tradition. Prophetic oracles collected from well over a century became part of Israel's scriptures as "Isaiah," to be read and reread in the centuries following the fall of Israel and Judah, the Exile, the restoration, and during the intervening centuries. Encompassed in the citation is not just a phrase from a literary work but a whole history of experience gathered around a pregnant text. While we cannot know all that the citation brought with it, we can learn a great deal—and the more we know, the richer the experience of the citation.

Those knowledgeable about the scriptures will, of course, immediately recognize that the citation is not only from Isaiah. It includes words from Malachi 3:1 and perhaps an echo of a passage from Exodus (23:20). That will not be a problem for readers of the King James Bible, since it introduces the citation in 1:2 as written "in the prophets." For those who use a contemporary text, however, the tension becomes apparent. How the passage about the "messenger" from Malachi came to be linked with the line from Isaiah is a topic for study. It may be that the writer of the Gospel had access to the scriptures as they had become part of

Christian tradition rather than as actual biblical texts. Such questions have generated a whole field of scholarship. Again, the more we know about the background of the scriptural passages, the more interesting they become.

Certainly knowledge of geography contributes to an appreciation of the story. That crowds throng to John in the "wilderness" around the Jordan is remarkable—not simply because the area is an unlikely setting for gathered crowds but because of the proximity to Jerusalem. Not far from where John is preaching is the religious center of the earth, according to many in Israel. Sacrifices for sin are offered daily. It is there, according to Psalm 132, that God promised he would dwell forever. So why do crowds have to come to the wilderness, outside the city, to "get religion"? A whole history of debate revolving around the Temple is conjured up—and it is hardly surprising when the Temple comes to be the center of the controversy that ends with Jesus' rejection and execution.

Some knowledge of John the Baptist is likewise helpful. The narrator presumes readers know something about the strange figure. We can learn more about John from the Jewish historian Josephus, who indicates that John was a person of political as well as religious importance.[2] During the first century, John was in fact more well known than Jesus.

One of the interesting details in Mark's account is the mention of John's clothing. In 2 Kings 1:8, we learn that Elijah the prophet wore such clothing. Elijah, according to 2 Kings 2:11, was taken to heaven alive in a chariot of fire. Elijah's future became a topic for discussion—and still is to this day. Even within Israel's scriptures there are expectations about Elijah. The prophet Malachi ends his oracles with a promise from God:

> Lo, I will send you the prophet Elijah before the great and terrible day of the LORD comes. He will turn the hearts of parents to their children and the hearts of children to their parents, so that I will not come and strike the land with a curse. (Mal 4:5-6)

For those who know the promise, John's appearance can be understood as Elijah's return. And when one's "Old Testament" ends with Malachi, the link is all the more significant.[3] Mark's story begins on the note on which Israel's scriptures end.

Even these few examples indicate how important to an appreciation of Mark's story knowledge of Israel's scriptures can be. Such knowledge is not necessary, but it contributes to a far richer experience of the story.

Other details are striking. The "tearing" of the heavens is one (presuming that English readers use a version that renders the Greek "tear" [NRSV] and not "open" [RSV]). Observant readers will note that the image appears once more in Mark's Gospel, at the conclusion of Jesus' ministry, at the moment of his death: "And the curtain of the temple was torn in two, from top to bottom" (15:38). Is there a relationship between the "tearing" of the heavens and the "tearing" of the temple curtain?

Translation again matters with regard to the comment about the descent of the Spirit. The NRSV translates, "he saw...the Spirit descending like a dove *on* him" (1:10). The translation is particularly unfortunate. While Matthew and Luke use "upon," the preposition in Mark is translated literally "into." Those who know Greek can appreciate why later in the story those who claim that Jesus is possessed by the ruler of demons are guilty of blasphemy against the Holy Spirit (3:22-30): Jesus is indeed possessed, but by the Spirit of God and not a demon. Something has indeed "gotten into him."

A final detail is the wording of the voice that speaks to Jesus from the torn heavens. The words are reminiscent of several important Bible passages. One is Psalm 2:7: "You are my son; today I have begotten you." The verse is actually quoted in Hebrews 1:5, in a passage discussing what it means that Jesus Christ has "become as much superior to angels as the name he has inherited is more excellent than theirs." Jesus, according to the passage cited by the author of Hebrews, is called "Son" by God. Knowledge of the history of this psalm in Jewish tradition provides an important setting for the whole Gospel. In the psalm, God speaks to his "anointed" (Messiah, Christ) and calls him "my son." Jesus is "Christ" and "Son of God." The titles have a history. Their setting within the royal tradition in Psalm 2 is a good place to begin.

"With you I am well pleased." The words are reminiscent of a famous passage from Isaiah 42:1:

> Here is my servant, whom I uphold,
> my chosen, in whom my soul delights;

> I have put my spirit upon him;
> he will bring forth justice to the nations.

While Mark's Greek is not a rendering familiar from the Septuagint, the wording is unmistakably from Isaiah. What it means—that Jesus receives the Spirit—is hinted at in these words reminiscent of Isaiah 42. As God's chosen and favored Son, he will bring justice to the nations. A script begins to emerge for the story.

At least as interesting is the reference to "beloved Son." The image is familiar from the story of Abraham and Isaac. Abraham is told, "Take your son, your only son Isaac, whom you love . . . and offer him there as a burnt offering . . ." (Gen 22:2). Does Jesus' destiny as a "beloved Son" have anything to do with the other? Traditions about the "Akedah," or "Binding of Isaac," have opened significant new vistas for readers of the NT.[4] The story of Abraham and Isaac, read in Jewish synagogues as the appointed text for Rosh Hashanah, the festival of the new year, may provide part of the setting for the story of another Father and Son.

None of this information is necessary to an appreciation of the passage. For the knowledgeable reader, however, the passage opens to new richness and depth.

THE IMAGINATIVE READER AND LISTENER

While close reading is necessary and knowledge helpful, the Gospel comes to life only as there is imaginative engagement. That is obvious at the most elementary level. The author provides few transitions. If the Gospel is to be experienced as a narrative, connections need to be supplied. We are not explicitly told, for example, that Jesus is the one of whom John speaks. At no point do we learn if John even knows that. Because the account of Jesus' baptism follows John's prophecy, however, we are inclined to make the connection. There is no great mystery here.

More interesting is what to make of some of the patterns in the narrative. For example, Jesus' story opens with the tearing of the heavens, the descent of the Spirit, and a declaration about his relationship to God as "Son." Jesus' ministry concludes with the same three elements, with some variation. It is the curtain of the temple that is torn, the Spirit leaves (Jesus "breathes out his spirit" [15:37 my translation), and a centurion makes a statement about Jesus as God's son (or Son). Even identifying the "pattern" suggests some creative involvement on the part of the interpreter, since nothing is explicitly said. Precisely how the initial events are related to the later is likewise not explicitly spelled out, and there are different possibilities. This is a place, in any case, where interpreters are required to exercise their imaginations.

What does it mean that the heavens are "being torn open" and the curtain of the Temple "was torn in two, from top to bottom"? Knowledge that the Temple was constructed as a microcosm may be suggestive. God is separated from his creation by a curtain— the one in front of the Holy of Holies as well as the "curtain" of the heavens. If it were not so, humans could not survive—for to stand in the presence of the holy God would mean death. What does it mean that the curtain is torn? It may mean that God is no longer one to be feared, that we have "access" to God. The Gospel story could then be construed as an account of how that access has been opened, with an implied invitation to enter. That seems to be the interpretation of the imagery offered by the author of the Letter to the Hebrews (Heb 9–10):

> Therefore, my friends, since we have confidence to enter the sanctuary by the blood of Jesus, by the new and living way he opened for us through the curtain (that is, through his flesh), and since we have a great priest over the house of God, let us approach with a true heart in full assurance of faith. (10:19-22)

I still recall the occasion when a young student protested that interpretation as I explained it. "That isn't what it means," he said vehemently. "It means that the protection is gone and now God is among us, on the loose." The imagery may as well suggest the removal of protection. The young man experienced the passage as dangerous. I have come to believe his experience is the more appropriate. Another of the Bible passages that might be echoed here is from Isaiah, who speaks about God's "rending the heavens and coming down" (64:1 RSV). The result will be judgment: the mountains will quake at God's presence. What would it mean if God were to remove the barriers and intrude into the "safe space" in which humans live? The story might then be imagined not as an invitation to come to God but as an account of how God has come into the world, with Jesus as the means by which God "intrudes."

Both interpretations are imaginative "leaps" without which the story remains inert. But which is then correct? That remains a question for interpreters. We must debate which produces the most satisfying reading—"satisfying" not simply as a psychological category but as something to be measured by adequacy to the narrative as judged by others with whom we read. For many reasons it seems to me more convincing that what drives the story is the problem that God comes too close in Jesus ("Who can forgive sins but God alone?").

A final question has to do with the relationship of Jesus' baptism to John's preaching. It might be argued that the narrator is simply naive about the potential impact of the story. Matthew deals explicitly with the problem that Jesus—the protagonist about whom extraordinary claims have already been made—should be baptized by John, who preaches a "baptism of repentance for the forgiveness of sins."

> Then Jesus came from Galilee to John at the Jordan, to be baptized by him. John would have prevented him, saying, "I need to be baptized by you, and do you come to me?" But Jesus answered him, "Let it be so now; for it is proper for us in this way to fulfill all righteousness." (Matt 3:13-15)

The dialogue between Jesus and John does not explain why it must be, simply that it is necessary "to fulfill all righteousness."

Mark's narrative opens questions rather than closes them. The story of Jesus Christ, the Son of God, begins with the main character where he ought not to be—among sinners being baptized by John. If he is the One who is to come, he ought to be elsewhere—in Jerusalem, for example. That he initiates his ministry outside the sacred precincts, among the unwashed, will characterize what follows. Jesus is never with the right people—something for which he is criticized. The story of the expected deliverer will end up on a cross: "He saved others, he cannot save himself" (15:31). And it will move out from an empty tomb. While Israel's tradition is drawn upon here, it is also dramatically altered in the face of the career of Jesus of Nazareth.

At the heart of the story we are to expect a surprise. The one who is to come appears, but in a way no one expects. And in the tension between what is expected and what occurs is a central feature of the story that we are told is "good news."

GREAT EXPECTATIONS

The function of story openings is to create expectations. Engagement requires expectations and hunches. The story may provide surprises, but even surprises depend upon a shared sense of what can be anticipated. For what kind of a story do the opening verses in the Gospel prepare us? I would suggest the following. The task of competent readers will be to offer an assessment of my suggestions, perhaps to offer others.

1. Mark's Gospel will argue a case. The story is told from the perspective of one who is persuaded that Jesus is the Messiah and Son of God, and that his story is the beginning of good news. What it means that Jesus is "Christ" and "Son of God," and what difference it makes that this is "good news" are the sorts of questions to which we may expect some answer.
2. The citation from Isaiah and the scriptural echoes in the voice at Jesus' baptism are particularly significant as introducing the "script" by which the story will proceed. The story is driven by a kind of necessity: it has been written or, to put it another way, it has been promised. That Jesus' career makes sense against the backdrop of ancient promises is an argument that will seek to win the adherence of the reader.
3. The form of the story—anonymous, third-person narrative—involves readers in a particular way. We are given a privileged position from the outset. We are not limited in the sense that any characters in the story are limited. We hear what God and unclean spirits say; we are given insight into scriptural passages that have a bearing on meaning; we learn what Jesus and others are thinking. The dynamics of involvement are very different from the case of stories told in the first person.

What we make of the story and how it affects us are related to the "insider status" imposed on us by the writer.

4. Jesus' entrance comes without any psychological preparation. What we learn of Jesus comes largely through hearing about his ministry, with an occasional scriptural reference or echo that sheds light on the events. Important are the social and political dimensions of the events—what happens, that is, when Jesus bursts onto the scene.

5. The image of the tearing heavens is best taken as a sign of an invasion rather than as an invitation to enter a sacred realm. God, enthroned in the distant heaven, chooses to come near in the presence of Jesus. The story is about a God who will not remain at a distance, who will not be domesticated in traditions or in a temple building. The tension and eventual violence are a direct response to this presence-of-God-come-too-near. The story can be appreciated, therefore, in terms of theophany, or the appearance of God. God is a character in the story. Without an accounting for God's presence and action, no interpretation can be deemed adequate.

6. Because the story makes claims about God's coming near, interpretation can rightly be expected to take seriously the ultimate claims made by the narrative, if not to render a verdict about the truthfulness of the story. That evaluation of truthfulness will include a sense of the effectiveness of the narrative as an argument. What happens when one is engaged by the Gospel? Does this engagement awaken or strengthen trust in God? Is the story "good news"? Such questions cannot be answered in advance but must await an encounter.

CHAPTER 2

THE
PLAYERS

The opening chapters of the Gospel introduce us to a host of characters. They include John the Baptizer and the crowds who flock to him; Jesus, who comes from Nazareth of Galilee to be baptized by John; Satan, who tests Jesus in the wilderness; God, who makes declarations from beyond the torn heavens; disciples, some of whom are named (Simon's sons, Simon and Andrew; the sons of Zebedee, James and John; and Alphaeus's son Levi), others who are not (Simon's mother-in-law and Simon's wife who is not even mentioned; the leper Jesus heals); unclean spirits; crowds; scribes and Pharisees.

More can be said about each of the groups. Much is taken for granted. Readers are given no background on John except that he wears camel hair and leather shorts. Associations with Elijah the prophet occur to those who know Israel's scriptures. John, a person of considerable influence, is introduced as Jesus' forerunner. A "stronger one" will come after him, to whom John points. Jesus' ministry begins on the ominous note of John's arrest (1:14), about which we learn nothing until a flashback several chapters into the story (6:17-29).

The Pharisees and scribes appear largely as stock characters interested in matters of purity. They are given no names; their characters have no depth. We learn only that they are concerned about Jesus' practice of eating with the unclean, doing things that may seem to dishonor the sabbath, and speaking and acting with an unwarranted authority. Jesus' claim to forgive sins, in fact, is regarded as blasphemy by the scribes, a foreshadowing of the charge on which Jesus will be declared guilty by the Jewish high court at the climax of the story.

While appreciating the role of these authority figures may require no more specific information than is provided, the difference between modern Western culture and traditional cultures, of which first-century Judaism is an example, invites some attention to the particulars.

PHARISEES, SADDUCEES, AND HERODIANS

The religious figures in Mark are carefully distinguished. Some terms designate an office: "scribes, chief priests, and elders" are officials, presumably in charge of the Temple and some governmental affairs in Jerusalem. "Pharisees" and "Sadducees" and "Herodians" are not official designations but identify parties within the community, much as denominational labels distinguish members of the Jewish and Christian family in terms of particular beliefs and traditions and practices. That Mark never explains titles indicates he expects readers to know what the labels mean.

Definitions of the terms are few. In a single instance, in an aside, Mark explains Pharisaic practice in a dispute about washing:

> For the Pharisees, and all the Jews, do not eat unless they thoroughly wash their hands, thus observing the tradition of the elders; and they do not eat anything from the market unless they wash it; and there are also many other traditions that they observe, the washing of cups, pots, and bronze kettles. (7:3-4)

We are given only a bit of information about Sadducees. In the context of an involved question about the resurrection of the dead Sadducees ask Jesus in 12:19-23, we are told that Sadducees "say there is no resurrection" (12:18). This fits the only other description of Sadducean practices in the New Testament, where we learn in Acts that "the Sadducees say that there is no resurrection, or angel, or spirit; but the Pharisees acknowledge all three" (Acts 23:8).

About "Herodians" we learn nothing.

What we know about Pharisees and Sadducees and Herodians

is limited to information provided by the New Testament, the historian Josephus, and a few references in later Jewish writings.[1]

In Mark, Pharisees are by far the most important of the groups. They appear throughout the opening half of the Gospel as religious people concerned with Jesus' apparent carelessness about ritual matters. Such concerns square well with what we know of the movement from other sources. Pharisees (whose name may mean "separate ones") appear around the time of the Maccabees, in the middle of the second century BCE, in response to the crises within the Jewish community brought about by efforts of Alexander the Great's successors to impose Greek ways on Israel by the use of force. To resist the rising tide of what they perceived to be paganism, Pharisees formed associations to observe the Law of Moses in a way that would preserve the distinctive features of their identity as the People of God and would provide an example to other Jews who were seduced by Greek culture. To interpret the Law in changing environments, they developed a tradition of legal interpretation known as the "oral law" or (as in Mark) the "tradition of the elders" (7:3). The remembered discussions of interpretation served as precedent in later legal discussions and decisions. In Mark's story, Pharisees are interested in careful observance of the sabbath, purity matters involving meals, and other important boundaries formed by the Torah.

The Sadducean movement was probably spawned during the same period in Israel's history as an alternative response to the same crisis. Mostly a priestly group, its members apparently resisted innovations from surrounding cultures that Pharisees embraced. They did not accept the Pharisees' "oral law." One of the characteristic views of Sadducees is that the idea of the resurrection of the dead does not belong to proper Jewish belief, which they measured primarily against what was written in the first five books of the Bible (Genesis through Deuteronomy). They appear in the New Testament as opponents of resurrection. The highly contrived question they pose about a woman who was married to seven brothers is designed to show that believing in the resurrection is incompatible with keeping the Law of Moses (Mark 12:18-27).

Christian tradition has tended to caricature Jewish piety and has fostered misunderstanding of the Pharisaic position. The concern among these pious Jews is not earning salvation; that is a gift of God. Nor is it to distance themselves from people they believe to be beneath them. Their goal is to take seriously what it means to have been called by God to be "a kingdom of priests and a holy nation." They believed that God gave the Law as a constitution for all of life. To sanctify daily life, they sought to apply the particular laws for priestly purity to all situations, like eating meals. To ensure that food was "kosher"—that is, proper food prepared according to scriptural instructions—and that the appropriate religious taxes had been paid, they were careful about their food and the people with whom they ate. They were likewise scrupulous about washing because they regarded mealtime as sacred and purity a sign of respect for God.

In their view Jesus was not careful enough. Observing the sabbath was a special concern in a Greek culture that did not respect the biblical commandment to rest on the last day of the week. Careful observance of the sabbath clearly distinguished Jews from their Gentile neighbors and thus provided an important identity marker. Mark tells a story in 3:1-6 about someone in the synagogue on the sabbath who appears with a physical defect. "They watched him to see whether he would cure him on the sabbath, so that they might accuse him" (3:2). The Pharisees did not believe the law forbids doing good on the sabbath, but the lack of clarity about what it means to "honor the sabbath day and keep it holy" required some discussion among legal experts about how to understand the scriptural prohibitions. In the *Mishnah*, the legal text of Rabbinic Judaism codified and written down around 200 CE, some things are allowed on the sabbath— like tying an umbilical cord at birth or performing a circumcision or burying the dead. People may seek to heal someone who is ill, but only if the illness is life-threatening. Differences of opinion existed. For the Pharisees, helping an animal that had fallen into a pit was not a violation of the sabbath. For those who lived on the shores of the Dead Sea and recorded their views in what we now know as the Dead Sea Scrolls, even helping an animal was considered forbidden. When Jesus takes up the issue in Matthew 10:11-12, he takes the position of the Pharisees.

Raising questions and disagreeing about what is allowed and what is not allowed on the sabbath is not unprecedented. Terming these discussions between Jesus and Pharisees "controversy stories" may lend an overly negative cast. Legal discussion involves differences of opinion. What is unusual here is that Jesus heals someone whose life is not threatened, and he does not cite precedent for his actions. He operates on his own authority, "and not like the scribes." It is the particular claim to stand above the tradition of the elders and to make pronouncements on his own authority that marks Jesus as dangerous.

Jesus' conversation partners, Pharisees in particular, view him as a potential social threat. By undermining respect for the law, Jesus is threatening not simply piety but social stability. Without boundaries communities cannot survive. When Jesus asks, "Who are my mother and brother and sisters?" he attacks the most basic unit of society. And when he uses the image of a bandit who breaks into people's houses as a way of speaking about his ministry ("No one can enter a strong man's house and plunder his property without first tying up the strong man; then indeed the house can be plundered" [Mark 3:27]), it is little wonder that respectable people become nervous.

SCRIBES, CHIEF PRIESTS, AND ELDERS

The group is mentioned for the first time in Jesus' prediction of what will occur in Jerusalem (8:31):

Then he began to teach them that the Son of Man must undergo great suffering, and be rejected by the elders, the chief priests, and the scribes. (8:31)

"Scribes" were trained interpreters of texts. "Elders" were lay leaders. "Chief priests" were members of aristocratic priestly families who provided leadership for the temple operation. Together, representatives of these groups formed the leadership in Jerusalem.

There is still considerable debate about the precise structure of leadership in Jerusalem in Jesus' day.[2] For interpreting Mark it is enough to note the clear distinction between the Jerusalem leaders and "Pharisees, Sadducees, and Herodians." Those who opposed Jesus in the fateful last days of his life are not identified in the story as "Israel," not even as Pharisees and Sadducees, but as an official body in charge of the Jerusalem government and the Temple. Jesus' controversy with them will prove fatal; they are the ones responsible for handing Jesus over to Pilate. The controversy that costs Jesus his life is principally with the religious authorities in Jerusalem. It is less clear in Mark how Jesus' earlier controversies with Pharisees are related to his trial before the Jewish leadership, the issues of which focus narrowly on the Temple and a messianic claim.[3]

SATAN AND UNCLEAN SPIRITS

A good bit of the drama in Mark's story arises from conflict between Jesus and unclean spirits. Jesus' first public action is to cast out an unclean spirit in a synagogue (1:21-27). Casting out demons is a regular feature of Jesus' ministry. When he commissions the Twelve, their call is "to be with him, and to be sent out to proclaim the message, and to have authority to cast out demons" (3:14-15). The view of unclean spirits and demons is different from Old Testament views and more like those of popular society within the Greco-Roman world. Evidence of demonic possession includes epilepsy-like symptoms (9:20-26), uncontrolled shouting (1:24; 5:7), superhuman feats of strength, and self-mutilation (5:2-5).

Early in the story, Jesus tells a "parable," in response to criticisms, that both interprets exorcisms and gives them a central place in his ministry:

And the scribes who came down from Jerusalem said, "He has Beelzebul, and by the ruler of the demons he casts out demons." And he called them to him, and spoke to them in parables, "How can Satan cast out Satan? If a kingdom is divided against itself, that kingdom cannot stand. And if a house is divided against itself, that house will not be able to stand. And if Satan has risen up against himself and is divided, he cannot stand, but his end has come. But no one can enter a strong man's house and plunder his property without first tying up the strong man; then indeed the house can be plundered." (3:22-27)

Heralding the kingdom of God involves asserting rights over against Satan's "kingdom." To use another image, within the household Jesus binds the strong man and drives out the dark forces. The battle for the world includes liberating those who are held in bondage by powers they are unable to control.

Little explanation of the demonic is offered. Understanding is presumed. How Satan's power is related to human agency, particularly in the last chapters of the Gospel, is never spelled out in detail. While in Luke Satan "enters" Judas, initiating the sequences of events that will result in Jesus' death, characters in Mark seem to play out their roles on their own. There are a few instances where language may suggest otherwise, but the author does not make the matter clear or consistent.

FAMILY

We are told remarkably little about Jesus' background, though as the story proceeds we learn a few bits of information. We learn, for example, that Jesus' hometown is Nazareth in Galilee. His status as a great healer and preacher contrasts with an apparently unremarkable background:

> On the sabbath he began to teach in the synagogue, and many who heard him were astounded. They said, "Where did this man get all this? What is this wisdom that has been given to him? What deeds of power are being done by his hands! Is not this the carpenter, the son of Mary and brother of James and Joses and Judas and Simon, and are not his sisters here with us?" (6:2-3)

It is strange that Jesus' father is not mentioned, but in other respects his background is quite ordinary. He has brothers (we know his brother James from the book of Acts and the apostle Paul) and sisters and a trade (carpenter). While Christian tradition has taken different views on Jesus' background, what is emphasized in Mark is its ordinariness. Knowing his past, people from his hometown are simply offended by his authority and power. Measuring by traditional standards, they can find no reason to believe that Jesus is remarkable. They are thus scandalized by his greatness.

The only other passage in which Jesus' relatives and family are mentioned is in chapter 3.

> Then he went home, and the crowd came together again, so that they could not even eat. When his family heard it, they went out to restrain him, *for they* were saying, "He has gone out of his mind." (3:19-21, my translation)

71

This is a passage in which translating is crucial. In 3:21, the NRSV presumes a change of subjects and translates, "for people were saying, 'He has gone out of his mind.'" Arguments for such a translation are not compelling. Without a clear indication of change in subject, the most natural reading is that Jesus' relatives go to get him because *they* believe he has lost his mind.

The evaluation of Jesus' relatives is followed by the assessment of the scribes that Jesus is possessed. That, in turn, is followed by a report about Jesus' more immediate family:

> Then his mother and his brothers came; and standing outside, they sent to him and called him. A crowd was sitting around him; and they said to him, "Your mother and your brothers and sisters are outside, asking for you." And he replied, "Who are my mother and my brothers?" And looking at those who sat around him, he said, "Here are my mother and my brothers! Whoever does the will of God is my brother and sister and mother." (3:31-35)

Again, we are to imagine that Jesus' family is worried about him and wants to take him home, away from the crowds. The statement about "true family," spoken while his immediate family is "outside," gives reason for the authorities' worry about Jesus. He seems unconstrained by traditional boundaries; even the family has no final status. What matters is doing the will of God—as Jesus defines it.

Jesus will have more to say about family matters—about marriage and children. About his own family, however, nothing more is said. They are among those who, like the scribes who attribute Jesus' power to demonic possession, are on the outside.

LITTLE PEOPLE

Mark's story is full of people whose names we never learn, many of whom are important because they are healed. There is the leper, the unnamed host who comes to Jesus for healing at sunset; Peter's mother-in-law who is healed and who rises to serve Jesus' group; the woman with a hemorrhage who touches Jesus' robe, confident that she will be healed; the daughter of the ruler of the synagogue (who is named—Jairus), a Gentile woman.

Unlike the authorities, these people come to Jesus believing that he can help. They are the least important members of their society—outcasts, people whose diseases have relegated them to the status of outsiders whom no one can even touch. Jesus' willingness to cross boundaries to touch and cleanse and eat with them brings life and hope where there was none. That willingness also threatens the whole religious and cultural and political system by which life is ordered. It is Jesus' concern for the little people that makes him a matter of concern to those who are in charge.

It is worthy of note that the categories by which these "outsiders" are declared outside are religious and not economic. Though we are introduced to a woman who had "endured much under many physicians, and had spent all that she had; and she was no better, but rather grew worse" (5:26), and another, a widow, whose meager contribution to the Temple treasury represents "everything she had, all she had to live on" (12:44), most of those Jesus deals with are defined as "out of bounds" by religious categories. The man with the unclean spirit, the leper, the possessed Gentile in the land of the Gerasenes, the woman with a hemorrhage, the Gentile woman who comes to beg for her daughter—these are all impure according to the standards of the law. The pious object because Jesus eats with "sinners and tax collectors."

One story in particular stands out. At a meal in the house of "Simon the leper," to whom we have not been introduced previously, an unnamed woman pours a jar of expensive ointment on Jesus' head. She is scolded by the guests who believe the gesture is wasteful. Jesus says to them:

> Let her alone; why do you trouble her? She has performed a good service for me. For you always have the poor with you, and you can show kindness to them whenever you wish; but you will not always have me. She has done what she could; she has anointed my body beforehand for its burial. Truly I tell you, wherever the good news is proclaimed in the whole world, what she has done will be told in remembrance of her. (14:6-9)

What is perhaps most remarkable about the story is that it is seldom told "wherever the good news is preached." The story has not been included in traditional lectionaries. That lack of attention in the face of Jesus' extravagant promise is one of the reasons Elisabeth Schüssler Fiorenza entitled her book *In Memory of Her: A Feminist Theological Reconstruction of Christian Origins.*[4]

On the one hand, these unimportant people turn out to be the only models of faith and discipleship in the story. Some have needs and the courage to ask for help. Others are beyond help and can be rescued only by Jesus' intrusion into their lives. They provide evidence that Jesus has the power to heal and drive out unclean spirits and that his ministry is indeed for those who are sick and in need. "Those who are well have no need of a physician, but those who are sick; I have come to call not the righteous but sinners" (2:17).

On the other hand, these scattered individuals have no impact on the direction of the story. As part of the larger crowds, they are simply swept up in the course of events. They have no power to alter the necessity that stands squarely in Jesus' path. Like everyone else, they are gone when the critical moment arrives and are finally as dependent as anyone else on God's intervention. They are as close to heroes as anyone in the story. But Mark's Gospel is not a story about heroes.

THE DISCIPLES

By far the most important characters in the story next to Jesus are the disciples. Their status is conferred: Jesus calls them. The accounts of that call are remarkably lacking in detail:

> As Jesus passed along the Sea of Galilee, he saw Simon and his brother Andrew casting a net into the sea—for they were fishermen. And Jesus said to them, "Follow me and I will make you fish for people." And immediately they left their nets and followed him. As he went a little farther, he saw James son of Zebedee and his brother John, who were in their boat mending the nets. Immediately he called them; and they left their father Zebedee in the boat with the hired men, and followed him. (1:16-20)

Jesus' followers are not confined to the Twelve. We hear of a larger group that asks about the parables, identified as "those who were around him along with the twelve" (4:10). That women are included in the larger circle of those who follow Jesus is noted in 15:40, where we are told that they "used to follow him and provided for him when he was in Galilee; and there were many other women who had come up with him to Jerusalem" (15:40-41). Specific names are mentioned (Mark 15:40, 47; 16:1).

74

"The Twelve," whose names are provided (3:16-19), represent an inner circle chosen from the larger group.

> He went up the mountain and called to him those whom he wanted, and they came to him. And he appointed twelve, whom he also named apostles, to be with him, and to be sent out to proclaim the message, and to have authority to cast out demons. (3:13-15)

Jesus creates a special group of insiders who are to share his own commission to preach, heal, and cast out demons. The occasion of their appointing—withdrawal to a mountain—suggests the significance of the actions; it also conjures up memories of notable events on mountains in Israel's past. The number twelve is surely suggestive of Israel's twelve tribes, though nothing explicit is said. Readers are apparently supposed to understand the significance of the numbers.

Some of the disciples are singled out as more significant than the others—simply because they function as an inner circle. Of particular importance are the two sets of brothers, Peter and Andrew, James and John. On many occasions Jesus explains things to the Twelve. On a few others, he brings along only the three (or four, including Andrew) and speaks to them (9:2-13; 13:3-36; 14:32-42). There are insiders, and there are real insiders. As readers, we are even more privileged, knowing what even Jesus' inner circle could not.

That the disciples are chosen and commissioned by Jesus, given special instruction and access to Jesus ("to you has been given the secret of the kingdom of God, but for those outside, everything comes in parables" [4:10-11]), and even enjoy success when sent out on their own, two by two, to preach and heal the sick (6:6-14), makes their performance in the story even more striking: the disciples do not understand. Their lack of comprehension early in the story ("Who then is this, that even the wind and the sea obey him?" [4:41]) yields neither to instruction nor experience. They seem impenetrable. They witness spectacular miracles, like the healing of the Gerasene demoniac and the two women (chap. 5). They participate in the miraculous feeding of multitudes with a few loaves—on one occasion, of five thousand people, on another, of four thousand. Yet in the second account, they expect no more than they did on the first occasion: "How can one feed these people with bread here in the desert?" they ask (8:4). When Peter finally shows signs of insight, confessing Jesus as "the Christ" (8:27-29), he immediately demonstrates how little he understands by rebuking Jesus—earning a rebuke himself: "Get behind me, Satan! For you are setting your mind not on divine things but on human things" (8:33).

We are pressed as readers to ask what the obduracy means. An interesting way to get at the issue is to ask how the disciples will be "played," whether as buffoons, simpletons, or even tragic figures. On the one hand, their dullness seems almost unfathomable. Jesus suggests one way of understanding lack of fruitfulness in his parable of the sower: there are many kinds of soil in which seed will never produce. Perhaps the disciples are simply poor soil. Such an explanation does not take seriously Jesus' initiative in choosing them, however. We must imagine there is something promising simply in the choice. And when the disciples are sent out to preach and heal in chapter 6, they are successful. Significant is the little comment by the narrator that "their hearts were hardened" (6:52), as well as Jesus' promises to the disciples that imagine a productive future (10:39-40; 13:10; 14:28-30).

The question to ask of the narrative, in view of the ending, is not simply whether the Jesus Movement has a future but if there is any hope for the disciples whom Jesus has chosen and to whom he has made promises. Is there reason to expect that life will spring up in the disciples and that they will bear fruit? If there is no future for them, there is little reason to imagine that Jesus' ministry has a future at all.

CHAPTER 3

WHO IS
GOD?

I f we are to identify as important characters those who are the focus of attention in the narrative, certainly Jesus and the disciples rank at the top. Apart from the opening account of the ministry of John the Baptist and the lengthy report of his death in 6:17-30, there is not a single scene in which Jesus is not present. The disciples—at least some of the disciples—are present through most of the story. Other characters—the Pharisees, Sadducees, scribes, chief priests, elders, crowds, the blind and possessed and deaf—move in and out of the story.

If by "important" we mean "rank," then a character who appears only irregularly in the story must emerge at the top: God.

Presuming that "Son of God" appears in the opening verse of the Gospel,[1] we may observe that God is introduced only in conjunction with Jesus. God is Jesus' implied "father." It works the other way as well: Jesus is important as the "son" of God (however the metaphor is to be understood). The frequency of "Son of God" suggests the term is important—and that the relationship between Jesus and "the Father" is critical for understanding both.

THE GOD OF ABRAHAM, ISAAC, AND JACOB

Perhaps the first thing to say is that the God who acts in the story and to whom Jesus is related as Son is the God of Israel. That is largely taken for granted. In at least two instances, however, it is explicitly spelled out:

> Have you not read in the book of Moses, in the story about the bush, how God said to him, "I am the God of Abraham, the God of Isaac, and the God of Jacob?" (12:26)

The point of the comment is not to inform the Sadducees about God's identity but to make a point based on the particular form of the statement ("I am...," not "I was..."). Jesus assumes his audience knows that he is speaking about Israel's God—the God of Abraham, Isaac, and Jacob.

The second passage, appearing only a few verses later, is a statement of the *Shema* from Deuteronomy 6:4, one of the most basic of Israel's confessions:

> Jesus answered, "The first [commandment] is, 'Hear, O Israel: the Lord our God, the Lord is one; you shall love the Lord your God with all your heart, and with all your soul, and with all your mind, and with all your strength.'" (12:29-30)

In response to the question of a lawyer, Jesus locates himself squarely in Israel's tradition. The God of whom he speaks and about whom the story speaks is the "Lord," the God of Abraham and Isaac and Jacob. That there are so few explicit statements to inform readers about this fact indicates that it is taken for granted.

Those familiar with the Hebrew scriptures of Israel—the Christian Old Testament—will know that Israel's God has a name. That the name does not appear in the New Testament is no surprise. God's mysterious name, transliterated into English from the Hebrew as YHWH, was no longer spoken aloud in the first century. In fact, uttering God's ineffable name was regarded as blasphemy. Hebrew readers of the scriptures read something else when they came to the name of God—most probably the word *Lord.* One would not know from Mark's Gospel—or in fact from the whole New Testament—that God has a special four-letter name. The matter is complicated by the fact that the New Testament is in Greek, and the scriptures of Israel read and studied by these New Testament communities were in Greek. The translation, known as the "Septuagint" (according to tradition, it was translated by seventy scholars, thus the name), had developed ways of dealing with God's name. Although there is evidence of old Greek manuscripts in which God's name is not translated but written in some ancient script, obviously to indicate that it is a name and cannot be translated, the New Testament seems to presuppose a Greek Old Testament that rendered the name of God with the ordinary Greek word *Lord*. The Greek version of Deuteronomy, cited in Mark 12:29-30, thus translates "YHWH our God, YHWH is one," as "the Lord our God, the Lord is one."

This little detour is important for understanding the use of "Lord" in English translations. Sometimes the word is used not as a title but as a proper noun, meaning "master": "so the Son of Man is lord even of the sabbath" (2:28); "What then will the owner [lit. "lord"] of the vineyard do?" (12:9). On other occasions it is a term of respect, best rendered "sir": "Sir ["lord"], even the dogs under the table eat the children's crumbs" (7:28). Most frequently it is the way one refers to God, as in 11:9, 12:11, 12:29, 13:20. The term is also used of Jesus, probably in light of the verse from Psalm 110:1: "The Lord said to my Lord, 'Sit at my right hand, until I put your enemies under your feet'" (Mark 12:36). Here the Lord God speaks to someone else the psalmist calls "Lord." According to Christians, this second "Lord" is the "Lord Jesus."

It is usually possible to distinguish between the "Lord God" and the "Lord Jesus" in Mark. In two places there is some question. The scriptural passage quoted in Mark 1:3 speaks about "preparing the way of the Lord." In its Old Testament setting, there is no question that the "Lord" here refers to God. In the context of Mark's Gospel it is less clear. John the Baptist prepares the way for one who comes after him. Perhaps we are already to think of Jesus as "Lord." If so, the language signals a departure from usual Jewish custom and a potentially dangerous usage. Improper use of God-language can mean blasphemy.

The other passage where "Lord" is ambiguous is in the story of the Gerasene demoniac. When the liberated demoniac asks to come with Jesus, Jesus tells him to return home and "tell them how much the Lord has done for you, and what mercy he has shown you" (5:19). The man, however, proclaims "how much Jesus had done for him" (5:20). Did the man misunderstand? Was Jesus referring to himself with language appropriate to God? The possible confusion becomes serious in a context where "the Lord our God, the Lord is one." Any compromising of that oneness of God means blasphemy. That happens to be the charge on which Jesus is finally condemned to death. In the eyes of some, at least, Jesus has crossed the boundary that separates the divine and the human.

THE GOD WHO ACTS

There are four events in the story in which God overtly "acts." Twice God speaks (1:11; 9:7) and twice God "tears." The pairs are related. In the baptismal scene, Jesus hears a voice from the heavens: "You are my Son, the Beloved; with you I am well pleased." At the Transfiguration, the inner circle of the disciples hears a voice that uses some of the same words: "This is my Son, the Beloved; listen to him!" Though the narrator does not explicitly identify God as the one who speaks, the scene leaves little doubt about the one who calls Jesus "Son."

In the baptismal scene, Jesus sees the heavens "being torn open"; at the moment of his death, the curtain of the Temple "is torn" from top to bottom. The passive voice may seem to leave open the subject of the sentences. Again, however, there is no doubt. The absence of the word *God* as the subject of the sentence probably reflects Jewish sensitivities: while only speaking the special name of God is expressly forbidden, it is a mark of respect to avoid using even the term "God," for which the passive voice may serve. It is God who tears away the heavens and who tears the Temple curtain "from top to bottom."

God's explicit actions have to do with barriers—the heavens and the curtain of the Temple. What they have in common is not simply their spatial referent but their function: both "curtains" protect humans from having to stand directly in the presence of God. In the story there is a breach in the protective barriers.

What the breach means and what it has to do with the presence of God are related to the use of "the Son of God." Jesus is the one in whom God is present in a world previously screened from that presence. What it means that God is no longer safely hidden behind the heavens or within the Temple remains to be seen.

On several other occasions, God's actions are concealed in the use of passive verbs.

4:10-12	"lest they turn and it *be forgiven* them" (my translation)
6:52; 8:17	"their hearts *had been hardened*" (my translation)
10:40	"but to sit at my right hand or at my left is not mine to grant, but it is for those *for whom it has been prepared*"
16:4	the stone *"had already been rolled away"* (16:4)
16:6	Jesus *"has been raised"* (16:6)

In all these passages, God is the implied subject of the sentence. God has rolled away the stone; God has raised Jesus. Perhaps the most difficult are the references to God's "hardening their hearts." The phrase has precedent in the Old Testament, the most famous being in the story of the Exodus when God hardens the heart of Pharaoh (Exod 10:1-2, 20, 27; 11:10). The use of the language here suggests that seeing and hearing and believing are not simply matters of human will. God makes such things possible. If God hardens the disciples' hearts, the question for the rest of the story is if God will liberate them.

"THE KINGDOM OF GOD"

If God's priority in the story were not clear, the frequency of the phrase "the kingdom of God" should point in that direction. Jesus' ministry begins with an announcement that the "Kingdom" is at hand. The translation of the Greek phrase has been a matter of dispute for a long time, and there is little evidence the debate will be settled anytime soon. The Greek *basileia* can be translated with a spatial force: "Kingdom" is a place, a sphere, a location where God rules. Or it may be translated as an activity: the "rule" of God, designating the activity more than the location or sphere. An older tendency to identify this "kingdom of God" with some institution, like the church, provoked a reaction. The active sense of "rule" avoids the need to identify precisely where this "Kingdom" is to be found.

In Mark the data is complex. While translating "the rule of God" seems to work in most instances, spatial imagery seems required on some occasions.

> And he called them to him, and spoke to them in parables, "How can Satan cast out Satan? If a kingdom is divided against itself, that kingdom cannot stand. And if a house is divided against itself, that house will not be able to stand." (3:23-25)

The paralleling of "house" and "kingdom" suggests one way of hearing "kingdom of God." Jesus' statement about binding the strong man and plundering his house seems to suggest a way of understanding his own ministry as the one who heralds the nearness of the kingdom of God (1:15). And Jesus' use of the image later in the story makes this more likely. When he uses the parable of the "master of the house" who appoints slaves to care for the house while he is away (13:33-37), there is some sense that "kingdom" as God's "rule" is an embodied activity and thus has a location.

Important here is that the "rule" or "kingdom" is God's rule or kingdom. Jesus is the herald. He may be more—perhaps the agent of its coming and establishment—but rule belongs finally to God. Whatever authority Jesus exercises is ultimately God's.

GOD AND THE LAW

God is important in the Gospel as the authority standing behind the Law of Moses.

> Then he said to them, "You have a fine way of rejecting the commandment of God in order to keep your tradition! For Moses said, 'Honor your father and your mother'; and, 'Whoever speaks evil of father or mother must surely die.' But you say that if anyone tells father or mother, 'Whatever support you might have had from me is Corban' (that is, an offering to God)—then you no longer permit doing anything for a father or mother, thus making void the word of God through your tradition that you have handed on."
> (Mark 7:9-13)

The issue is a dispute about interpreting versions of the fourth commandment (see Exod 21:17; Deut 5; Lev 20:9). The practice of designating money as "Corban" is a Pharisaic practice. It is considered part of special duty to God. At issue is not motivation but legitimacy of interpretation: Is the dedication of funds to God really a sign of special piety, or does it constitute disobedience to the commandment about honoring one's parents, since the money set aside would not be available for parental support? These are the sorts of issues that separated various observant groups within the Jewish community—like Sadducees, Pharisees, and Essenes. Such disputes indicate that the Law is significant only as it is practiced, and that practice always involves interpretation.

The same point is made in the controversy about divorce.

> Some Pharisees came, and to test him they asked, "Is it lawful for a man to divorce his wife?" He answered them, "What did Moses command you?" They said, "Moses allowed a man to write a certificate of dismissal and to divorce her." But Jesus said to them, "Because of your hardness of heart he wrote this commandment for you. But from the beginning of creation, 'God made them male and female.' 'For this reason a man shall leave his father and mother and be joined to his wife, and the two shall become one flesh.' So they are no longer two, but one flesh. Therefore what God has joined together, let no one separate." (Mark 10:2-9)

The passage presumes that God is the author of the Law and that it is to be obeyed. The particular issue surrounding divorce came to focus on a discussion of Deuteronomy 24:1-2:

> Suppose a man enters into marriage with a woman, but she does not please him because he finds something objectionable about her, and so he writes her a certificate of divorce...

The passage presumes that under certain circumstances divorce is permitted to husbands. The question is, Under precisely what circumstances? That depends upon the interpretation of the phrase "something objectionable." There were disputes among Jewish teachers about the permissible scope of divorce, with one group arguing for a restrictive view ("something objectionable" means "infidelity and adultery") and the other for a broader view ("something objectionable" means "anything displeasing"). Both groups presume the authority of the Law, and both recognize that the Law requires interpretation.

Precisely how to interpret—and who has the authority to interpret—is present in the question put to Jesus.

> What God has joined together, let no one separate. (10:9)

Jesus offers a reading that seeks to clarify the ambiguous term by appeal to the primary "intention" of God from Genesis: "The two shall become one flesh. What God has joined together, let no one separate." Other biblical passages that seem to suggest it is appropriate to divorce are here understood as concessions due to "hardness of heart." His interpretation of the Law, while more stringent than that of either school of Pharisees, remains within the scope of proper interpretation.

God is not simply the Creator of the heavens and the earth, but the author of the Law by which life is regulated and structured. God "joins together" through the agency of the Law. Interpretation is very much part of divine activity, since it is the way God's Law takes concrete shape. And interpretation necessarily raises questions of authority. Who has the right to interpret—and thus to speak for God?

Disputes about purity laws—for example, sabbath observance, food laws—presume that the Law of Moses is God's law and that the community for which Mark writes has a stake in that Law. The major difference between Mark's Gospel and the later Jewish Law Codes, like the Mishnah, is formal: legal issues are not settled through debate and voting. Jesus makes pronouncements. The law must be interpreted—but it is Jesus who has the authority to interpret, even to speak for God.

God's "work" through the Law is thus embodied in Jesus and not in the "tradition of the elders." The question will thus be: "By what authority are you doing these things?" (11:28). And the charge against Jesus within the Jewish community is that he arrogates too much authority to himself: he blasphemes.

GOD'S FUTURE WORK

> Then Jesus said to them, "The cup that I drink you will drink; and with the baptism with which I am baptized, you will be baptized; but to sit at my right hand or at my left is not mine to grant, but it is for those for whom it has been prepared." (10:39-40)

"But about that day or hour no one knows, neither the angels in heaven, nor the Son, but only the Father." (13:32)

These passages are among those that envision a future in which God will play a decisive role. Only "the Father" knows the exact time of the end. It is God who "has prepared" who will sit at Jesus' right hand and his left (on the use of the passive, see above). The language suggests that God has planned the course of the future.

GOD THE FATHER

The image of God as "Father" has had a great impact on the language of the church. It is a term familiar from the Old Testament but not common in postbiblical Judaism. Mark's Gospel includes no version of the Lord's Prayer, and on only a few occasions is God identified as "Father." What it means to refer to God as "Father" thus merits some comment.

Perhaps the major reason for using the parental metaphor for God is that Jesus is regularly called "Son of God." Twice in the Gospel God explicitly calls Jesus "my Son" (1:11; 9:7). Demons regularly identify Jesus as "the Son of God." On only one occasion does Jesus address God as "Father"—in Gethsemane, where he uses the Aramaic "Abba" (translated immediately by the Greek). On another occasion Jesus speaks of God as "the Father": "But about that day or hour no one knows, neither the angels in heaven, nor the Son, but only the Father" (13:32). Only once does Jesus speak of God as the father of anyone else:

Whenever you stand praying, forgive, if you have anything against anyone; so that your Father in heaven may also forgive you your trespasses. (11:25)

Significant is the relative infrequency of the language and the restricted use of the metaphor. God is spoken of almost exclusively as Jesus' "Father." Despite the one reference to "your Father in heaven," no one is invited to address God as "Father" or "our Father." In the Gospel narrative, in other words, the image of God as "Father" is appropriate to Jesus as "Son." That Jesus' followers can understand themselves as "sons" (or "children") of God the Father is never stated explicitly, though "your Father in heaven" may imply it.

The closest we come to a sense of the metaphor is in the use of biblical allusion in the voice from heaven (1:11). "My son" is what God calls the King, his "anointed" (2:2) in Psalm 2:

> He who sits in the heavens laughs;
>   the LORD has them in derision.
> Then he will speak to them in his wrath,
>   and terrify them in his fury, saying,
> "I have set my king on Zion, my holy hill."
> I will tell of the decree of the LORD:
> He said to me, "You are my son; today I have begotten you.
> Ask of me, and I will make the nations your heritage,
>   and the ends of the earth your possession.
> You shall break them with a rod of iron,
>   and dash them in pieces like a potter's vessel." (vv. 4-9)

"Son of God" is royal terminology, as we know from 2 Samuel 7:14 (RSV): "I will be his father, and he shall be my son." Psalm 2, like 2 Samuel 7:14, was by the first century read as an oracle in which God speaks not about any historical figure but about the Messiah-King from the line of David. "Son of God" thus defines the relationship of Jesus to God as the Christ (or Messiah).

God is "Father," therefore, as related to Jesus as "Son." The language suggests that God has something invested in Jesus' career. The metaphor does not take as its point of departure the ordinary experience of fathers in human families. And that God is called "Father" by anyone but Jesus, or addressed in prayer as "Abba" by anyone but Jesus the Son, is not made clear in Mark's Gospel. The use of "your Father in heaven" in the context of prayer (11:26) may suggest the currency of such language, perhaps following a Pauline argument, that those who are "in Christ" may call God "Father" (Galatians 3).

CHAPTER 4

WHO IS
JESUS?

The question may seem both too simple and too large. The story is all about Jesus, and it would seem obvious who he is. Groups tend to answer the question in very different ways, however, both among contemporary readers and within the Gospel narrative. On the contemporary scene, some see the narrative through the lens of suspicion, convinced that in important ways Mark's Gospel distorts the truth about Jesus. The Jesus Seminar is only the most current manifestation of a reading strategy begun in the eighteenth century in which the task of the reader is to move critically behind the Gospel story to the "facts" about Jesus. Such reconstructions include portraying Jesus as a deluded fanatic; an unfortunate victim of political power plays; a moral man whose most revolutionary act was to eat with sinners and tax collectors; and a Galilean healer/exorcist with affinities to particular Jewish or Greco-Roman types.

The variety of response among current readers of the Gospel has clear precedent: viewing his ministry, Jesus' contemporaries were by no means agreed about what to make of him. The current debate thus provides a useful entrée to the story where everyone seems to have a different opinion about Jesus. Understanding Jesus must include some sense of what various groups make of him and why there is such controversy. We begin, therefore, with the question Jesus asks of his disciples and their response.

"WHO DO PEOPLE SAY THAT I AM?" DIFFERING APPRAISALS

Jesus went on with his disciples to the villages of Caesarea Philippi; and on the way he asked his disciples, "Who do people say that I am?" And they answered him, "John the Baptist; and others, Elijah; and still others, one of the prophets." He asked them, "But who do you say that I am?" Peter answered him, "You are the Messiah."

(8:27-29)

An important aspect of Jesus' identity is how people react to him. The answer to the question "Who, then, is this?" depends on who is asked. When the disciples tell Jesus what people think of him at the midway point in the Gospel—"John the Baptist, Elijah, one of the prophets"—as readers we are aware they are only telling part of the story. That the Gospel takes so much time depicting the reaction of a wide variety of groups to Jesus suggests that the matter is worth noting. While the readers' impression of Jesus will be different from that of any of the characters in the story, the impression will surely be shaped by what others think.

Family

The primary group within which identity is formed and located is the family. That was surely the case in the ancient world. It is significant that Jesus' relatives, including his mother, brothers, and sisters, apparently do not appreciate his work. We are told that relatives seek to "restrain him" because they believe he is out of his mind (3:20-21). As noted earlier, in the same context we are told that Jesus' immediate family tries to summon him:

Then his mother and his brothers came; and standing outside, they sent to him and called him. A crowd was sitting around him; and they said to him, "Your mother and your brothers and sisters are outside, asking for you." And he replied, "Who are my mother and my brothers?" And looking at those who sat around him, he said, "Here are my mother and my brothers! Whoever does the will of God is my brother and sister and mother." (Mark 3:31-35)

Particularly in traditional societies, such a statement about families would be heard as radical. If there are those on the inside, Jesus' family is surely not included. Who Jesus is does not depend upon his family membership. In fact, it appears that identity may be formed over against traditional families.

Pharisees

As noted above, the Pharisees—pious, observant Jews—are troubled by Jesus' lack of care about observing the law. They raise questions about his religious practices, like eating with sinners and tax collectors, not fasting, and being careless about sabbath observance. Their concern about his behavior leads to early speculation about how to get rid of him (3:6).

Scribes

When Jesus saw their faith, he said to the paralytic, "Son, your sins are forgiven." Now some of the scribes were sitting there, questioning in their hearts, "Why does this fellow speak in this way? It is blasphemy! Who can forgive sins but God alone?" (2:5-7)

And the scribes who came down from Jerusalem said, "He has Beelzebul, and by the ruler of the demons he casts out demons." (3:22)

While the pious question Jesus' interpretation of the Law, scribes charge Jesus with possible blasphemy, a capital crime. The same scribes, religious authorities who come down from Jerusalem (the first we hear of Jerusalem), also offer an evaluation of Jesus. They cannot deny his power. They attribute it, however, to spirit possession. They are correct—but it is the Holy Spirit who inhabits Jesus, not the Prince of Demons. It is they, not Jesus, who are guilty of blasphemy (3:28-30).

Herod

> King Herod heard of it, for Jesus' name had become known. Some were saying, "John the baptizer has been raised from the dead; and for this reason these powers are at work in him." But others said, "It is Elijah." And others said, "It is a prophet, like one of the prophets of old." But when Herod heard of it, he said, "John, whom I beheaded, has been raised." (6:14-16)

The little appraisal that introduces the account of John's beheading offers an estimate repeated in 8:27-29: the people believe Jesus to be a prophet. Herod fears that John the Baptist, the troublemaker he had beheaded, has been raised. The image of a prophet like Elijah or Moses, miracle-working prophets whose return was predicted in the scriptures, seems to be one appropriate estimate of Jesus' work. Given the kinds of stories told about Jesus, people's views are not surprising. The people and Herod have different responses to Jesus' possible identity, however. Herod is afraid; the people rejoice.

The Common People

The common people flock to Jesus. They are identified not principally in political or economic categories but medical: they are sick and possessed. They come to listen ("for he taught them as one having authority, and not as the scribes" [1:22]) and to be healed. The people themselves use no titles in referring to Jesus, but the twice-repeated comment that people believe Jesus to be a prophet offers the appropriate evaluation.

Upon closer examination the parallels between Jesus and the prophets Elijah and Elisha are striking. It is not simply Jesus' authority but the wonders he performs. He brings a young girl back to life (Mark 5:21-43). Similar stories are told about Elijah and Elisha (1 Kgs 17:17-24; 2 Kgs 4:17-37). He feeds a large group with a little bread and has some left. The two feeding stories are reminiscent of the manna in the wilderness but are perhaps even more similar to a story told about Elisha (2 Kgs 4:42-44).

The evaluation of Jesus as prophet depends not simply upon observed similarities to biblical figures. In Israel's visions and dreams of the future, people expected a "prophet like Moses" (Deut 18:16-20) or Elijah (Mal 4:5-6) to come at the end of days. Identifying Jesus as a prophet suggests an impressive evaluation,

90

since according to most traditions there were no longer prophets in Israel and would not be until the end of days. Believing Jesus to be a prophet thus means believing some great era in history is dawning ("the kingdom of God is at hand").

The Disciples

We shall have opportunity to study the disciples in more detail. While their place as insiders is never in question, many of their early responses to Jesus suggest bewilderment and confusion: "Who then is this, that even the wind and the sea obey him?" (4:41). They regularly address Jesus as "teacher." It is only the disciples—in fact, only Peter—who ever suggest that Jesus is the Messiah (8:29).

Supernatural Beings

Supernatural characters—both demons and God—have opportunity to offer their evaluations. On the two occasions when God speaks, Jesus is identified as "my Son." As we have seen, the language of divine sonship belongs first within the context of royal language. The two Old Testament passages that are particularly relevant as background are Psalm 2:7 and 2 Samuel 7:14. In both passages, God addresses the king as "son." Equally important, both of these passages became part of Israel's vision of the future. They were understood to refer, in other words, to the promised Messiah-King who would arise at the end of days.

The setting within royal tradition seems a good introduction to the language unclean spirits use to address Jesus. They speak of him as "the Holy One of God," "the Son of God," and "the Son of the Most High God." This aspect of Jesus' identity appears to be obscured from human participants in the drama. No human being echoes the evaluation of the demoniacs. It is only the chief priest who addresses Jesus as "the Christ, the Son of the Blessed [i.e., God]" (14:61 RSV) and the centurion who refers to Jesus as "God's Son" (or God's son) (15:39). In the context of the passion story, the royal imagery dominates, suggesting that "Son of God" belongs within that constellation of images (see below).

The Scribes, Chief Priests, and Elders

This particular group appears for the first time in Jesus' initial prediction of his death and resurrection.

> Then he began to teach them that the Son of Man must undergo great suffering, and be rejected by the elders, the chief priests, and the scribes. (8:31)

They are the ones who will "reject" him. We are told that "they were afraid of him, because the whole crowd was spellbound by his teaching" (11:18). They are committed to arresting Jesus, but they fear his popularity, so they must find a way "by stealth" (14:1-2). Judas Iscariot gives them their opportunity when he leads them to Jesus as he is alone with his followers in the Garden of Gethsemane.

The trial before the Jewish authorities is one of the central moments in the story. Jesus is accused of having spoken against the Temple. The chief priest explicitly asks Jesus if he is "the Christ, the Son of the Blessed" (14:61 RSV). With Jesus' response, "I am; and 'you will see...'"(14:62), the court condemns him to death for blasphemy and then hands him over to Pilate.

Pilate

Pilate's sole role is to play a part in Jesus' death. For Pilate, Caesar's representative, the charge that Jesus claims to be "the King of the Jews" is a political matter. Such a claim implies sedition in Caesar's dominion. While the account of Jesus' trial before Pilate allows for a certain ambivalence on Pilate's part, he finally gives the command to have Jesus executed. The soldiers' mock investiture of Jesus, dressing him in a robe with a crown of thorns, offers their estimate of his identity. From their point of view, the claim that he is king is a joke, and they make fun at his expense.

"BUT WHO DO YOU SAY THAT I AM?" A READER'S EVALUATION

We do not read the Gospel from the perspective of any of the characters. We can appreciate all of their perspectives and that of the narrator as well. The story is not a neutral description of Jesus' career. It is an argument that intends to move readers. While readers may react differently, it is possible to appreciate features of the argument the Gospel seeks to make.

The most obvious "argument" is that Jesus is the Christ and Son of God. The opening line of the Gospel states the matter simply: "The beginning of the gospel of Jesus Christ, the son of God" (1:1 RSV). We have already looked at aspects of this verse. It may be obvious, but it is worth stating that from the outset Jesus is portrayed not as an exemplary figure but as someone singular and particular. His is not a story about the ideal human. He is identified by titles: Christ, Son of God, Holy One of God, prophet, teacher, Son of David. The titles refer to specific figures in Jewish visions and dreams of the future (see "What Language Shall We Borrow" at the end of this chapter). Even without clarity about their precise meaning, the use indicates that Jesus is special.

When he is baptized at the hands of John the Baptizer—in every sense like other "sinners"—the heavens are torn open; his death occasions the tearing of the Temple curtain. Both events mark a decisive transition. The Jesus who strides through the Gospel is acknowledged by demons as *the* Son of God, *the* Holy One of God. He dies not as a typical martyr or sufferer but as "the Christ, the Son of the Blessed One," "the Christ, the King of Israel," "the King of the Jews." He claims the authority to forgive sins, presumably on God's behalf, and is finally condemned for blasphemy. The titles are various ways of attesting to Jesus' singularity. Discipleship will have particular consequences, but not because Jesus reveals a "way" that others are to emulate. He is not simply a revealer. He is a singular deliverer. In addition to being named Jesus, being from Nazareth, having a mother named Mary and brothers and sisters, the Gospel claims that Jesus is "the Christ, the Son of God."

Jesus' credentials do not include an account of his heritage or birth or youth or call. We meet Jesus as an adult who comes to John for baptism. The only introduction we are given in the narrative, apart from the opening line, is in the biblical words (from Isaiah and Malachi) in which a messenger is to go before *you* to prepare *your* way. While we learn immediately that John's is the "voice of one crying in the desert," the identity of this "you" is simply implied.

There is further introduction of Jesus in the words of the Baptist:

> The one who is more powerful than I is coming after me; I am not worthy to stoop down and untie the thong of his sandals. I have baptized you with water; but he will baptize you with the Holy Spirit. (Mark 1:7-8)

The only reason we know John is speaking about Jesus is that we have been given to expect from 1:1 that the story is about Jesus—and immediately after John's speech we are told of his arrival. This particular juxtaposition is revealing, however. While John promises that the stronger one who comes after him will "baptize you with the Holy Spirit," Jesus does no baptizing but is himself baptized by John. Why that should be necessary—and when he will himself baptize—is left unanswered as the narrative continues. Interpreting Mark will involve making sense of the surprises as well as asking what to make of the unfulfilled promises that continue to mount as the story unfolds.

That Jesus is God's Son is confirmed by the voice from heaven: "You are my Son, the Beloved; with you I am well pleased." The descent of the Spirit "into him, like a dove," provides the motive power for his ministry.

Jesus begins his ministry upon John's arrest, an indication of what is to come, with a simple message:

> The time is fulfilled, and the kingdom of God has come near; repent, and believe in the good news. (Mark 1:15)

Healing and Liberation: "Plundering Satan's House"

Jesus is a preacher, but not simply a preacher. His mission is first of all one of healing. Typical of Mark, the opening scene in his public ministry is set in a synagogue in which Jesus has a confrontation with unclean spirit. His ministry will consist principally of action—casting out demons, healing the sick. We shall examine various accounts of Jesus' ministry of liberation in another chapter.

Metaphors are significant. They provide ways to gather together various strands of the story. Jesus preaches that the "kingdom of God has come near." What kind of metaphor is "kingdom of God"? The term is never defined, suggesting an audience that understands the language. Without specialized knowledge, how are ordinary readers to understand the expression? A significant passage for understanding both the image and its relationship to Jesus' ministry is Jesus' response to the accusation of the scribes that he is possessed:

> And the scribes who came down from Jerusalem said, "He has Beelzebul, and by the ruler of the demons he casts out demons."

And he called them to him, and spoke to them in parables, "How can Satan cast out Satan? If a kingdom is divided against itself, that kingdom cannot stand. And if a house is divided against itself, that house will not be able to stand. And if Satan has risen up against himself and is divided, he cannot stand, but his end has come. But no one can enter a strong man's house and plunder his property without first tying up the strong man; then indeed the house can be plundered." (3:22-27)

"Kingdom" is here paired with "household." It is viewed as a sphere in which some authority is in charge. Implied is that Satan is in charge of the household and that any change in authority will involve a struggle for power. Taking over will involve "binding the strong man." We have already learned from John the Baptist that Jesus is the "stronger one." The metaphors suggest that Jesus is not simply the herald of the impending kingdom of God; he is the agent. If God is to rule—to preside over the household, to use the imagery—someone will have to be bound. In his exorcisms, Jesus is wresting control from Satan by binding the unclean spirits and driving them out.

The image of "plundering the household" is particularly striking. It refers to acts of deliverance that will characterize Jesus' ministry—but it also views those activities from the perspective of the established authorities. Jesus will be accused of "breaking and entering." He intrudes into places where his authority is contested. His advent will be marked by family discord and social disruption. Those in authority will view this as socially (and religiously and politically) risky behavior. From the perspective of those in bondage, this "plundering" is liberation and salvation.

The imagery provides a way to understand Jesus' ministry of healing and exorcism and the conflict it engenders, for he contests the lordship of established powers not only at the mythic level (Satan and the unclean spirits) but also at the social and political levels. It is the religious and political leaders who will finally have to make a judgment about the "household" over which they preside and for which they are to exercise care. They will be forced to judge between Jesus and the well-being of families, the Temple, and the political order. Early in the story we have a sense of what they will decide.

The Teacher

Jesus is called "teacher" more frequently in Mark than in any of the other Gospels. Yet the actual teaching of Jesus included in Mark is the least of all the Gospels. Jesus' ministry is about action. His actions occasion controversy, however, and one aspect of his teaching is response to pious Jews who raise questions about his practice. Jesus' brief statements about his association with sinners and tax collectors, healing on the sabbath, and his carelessness about ritual matters offer interpretations of his ministry. "New skins for new wine," he tells his critics (2:22). And the common people are impressed. "He taught them as one having authority, and not as the scribes" (1:22).

Teaching occurs in large blocks in the Gospel, the first of which occurs in chapter 4, made up largely of parables. While delivered to the crowds, the parables are of particular significance for the disciples, the "insiders" whom Jesus has selected. Jesus must explain the little stories to his disciples; outsiders get only the parables (or "riddles"). This aspect of the parables will be considered in greater depth in the discussion of secrecy.

The "parables," extended analogies drawn from agricultural life, speak about the kingdom of God in terms of planting and harvesting, seeds and full-grown plants. The immediate setting is Jesus' announcement that "the kingdom of God is at hand," followed by activity that is impressive to some, less to others. The contrasts between beginning and end, small and large, relate the humble beginnings of Jesus' ministry to a promised conclusion.

While historical study of the parables seeks to understand what they meant as actually spoken by Jesus, abstracted from their setting in the Gospel story, more current scholarship reads the parables within the context of the ministry Mark sketches.

The second major collection of Jesus' teaching follows Peter's confession and Jesus' first announcement that he is headed for rejection and death in Jerusalem. The theme of the loosely tied instruction is discipleship: "Let those who would come after me deny themselves, take up their crosses, and follow." The topics include reflection on "greatness," usually in response to disciples who seem preoccupied with their status; discussion about divorce and the importance of children, instruction about abandoning wealth, and the rewards for those who do (see below).

The last block of instructional material is an extended response to Peter, James, John, and Andrew that develops Jesus' prediction about the impending destruction of the Temple and Jerusalem (Mark 13). The passage, often called the "little apocalypse" in light of its revelatory character and its use of visionary materials from Daniel, offers a glimpse of what can be expected in the near future. The chapter seems clearly to presume that Jerusalem will be destroyed, and it sees these events as triggering a larger chain of events that will lead to Jesus' triumphant return. While the chapter raises intriguing historical questions, it plays a crucial role in introducing the story of Jesus' death and is worth examining in some detail.

Crossing Boundaries: Jesus and the Law

Another feature of the Gospel's construction of Jesus' ministry has to do with boundaries. The world into which Jesus comes is one with clear lines separating clean and unclean, righteous and unrighteous, appropriate and inappropriate. From the very beginning Jesus is depicted as someone who crosses the lines. While "Son of God," his ministry begins with his baptism at the hands of John who preaches a "baptism of repentance for the forgiveness of sins." One of his first acts is to touch a leper, an act dangerous to those who are well and forbidden by the Law of Moses. He regularly invites to his table "sinners and tax collectors," people who for various reasons were regarded as unclean. He is careless about sabbath observance. He visits the unclean land of the Gerasenes and deals with unclean spirits among tombs with a herd of swine nearby.

The issue is complex. Jesus is not depicted as unobservant. Pharisees respect him, which is why they express amazement at some of his practices. Likewise the problem is not the Law of Moses. God is its author, and Jesus' life is lived largely within its bounds. That makes the boundary-crossings all the more serious.

The clearest boundary drawn by the Law is that between Creator and creature. Transgressing this boundary is called blasphemy—infringing on God's prerogatives. This boundary is protected by the most severe penalties. Those who commit blasphemy are to be stoned to death (Lev 24:10-16). Early in his ministry Jesus is accused of blasphemy for presuming to forgive sins. The charge on which he is convicted before the Jewish court is blasphemy: "'You have heard his blasphemy! What is your decision?' All of them condemned him as deserving death" (14:64 RSV).

Understanding Jesus will include appreciating the boundaries and their importance, as well as Jesus' apparent commitment to cross them in pursuit of God's will.

"Born to Die"

Perhaps the most significant thing about Jesus is that he will die. That becomes clear from the earliest moments in the story. As the preparer of the way, John the Baptizer is arrested—and as we learn, martyred—by the authorities. In the shadow of his arrest, Jesus begins his own ministry, which will end on a Roman cross. How he gets there—and what it means that he is crucified—is one of the major themes of the narrative. That Jesus' death is important in understanding his ministry should be obvious simply from the proportion of the story devoted to his arrest, trial, and death. More than a third deals with his last week, and a full sixth of the Gospel is devoted to his last twenty-four hours. The shadow of the cross is cast over the whole story, however, since accusations and plots begin almost immediately. To understand Jesus means not only to know that he died but why and what the implications are.

Equally important is that Jesus' death occurs according to the will of God. In the first prediction of his passion, Jesus uses the word *necessary* to characterize what will occur. The notion that "the Son of Man goes as it is written of him" (14:21) suggests the same inevitability. Jesus' prayer, "Abba, Father, for you all things are possible; remove this cup from me; yet, not what I want, but what you want" (14:36), suggests that things might be otherwise. God's silence, however, and the immediate arrival of the soldiers suggest that this is what God "wants." Understanding Jesus' death thus means also understanding the event as carried out according to the will of God.

ᏅᎵᎥᎧ   ᏅᎵᎥᎧ   ᏅᎵᎥᎧ   ᏅᎵᎥᎧ

WHAT LANGUAGE SHALL WE BORROW? A BRIEF REFLECTION ON TITLES

A traditional way of answering the question "Who is Jesus?" is to focus on the titles used to speak of him. They would include

"Christ" ("Messiah" in the NRSV), "Son of God" (with the variants "Son of the Most High God" [5:7], and "Son of the Blessed One" [14:61]), and "the Holy One of God" (1:24). "One of the prophets" and "Elijah" (8:28) are not titles, but they designate a prophetic office that might be included with "Christ" ("Messiah"). As we have noted, it is possible to understand much of what the terms mean from the narrative setting. Specialized knowledge is not required. It is not a disadvantage to know something of the background of the terms, however. Whole books are written on such matters, which indicates that the evidence from the world of the New Testament is relevant. The multiple volumes also suggest the evidence does not yield a consistent picture. Nevertheless, there are some things about which there is agreement that can be of help in understanding the use of specialized terms in the Gospel. Some study of the background of the language is helpful in any case, because most Bible readers have some sense of what terms like "Christ" ("Messiah") mean—and their knowledge may well be incorrect and thus distorting.

We have already examined some of the Old Testament background for "Son of God." Here I will discuss "the Christ" (or the Messiah) and "the Son of Man."

"The Christ" ("The Messiah")

The term most familiar to "Christ-ians" will be "Christ." Judging from the opening verse, readers would have no idea the Greek *Christos* is a title. It looks like Jesus' second name. Reading on, we discover that it is actually a title. Peter confesses, "You are the Christ" (8:29 RSV); the chief priest asks, "Are you the Christ, the Son of the Blessed?" (14:61 RSV); those who mock Jesus call him, "the Christ, the King of Israel" (15:32 RSV). The term seems to designate an office. All sorts of questions arise from noting the usage. One is how the title came to be part of Jesus' name.

English readers may have reason for some confusion. The NRSV has chosen to translate the Greek *Christos* (lit., "anointed one") as "Messiah," even though the English term is simply a transliteration of the Hebrew *Mashiach*. The reason is to make English readers aware that "Christ" is not "Christian" terminology but Jewish. The fact is that Jews spoke Greek as well as Hebrew; they read their Bible in Greek (the Septuagint) as well as in Hebrew, so that "Christ" and "the Christ" are as Jewish as "the Messiah."

99

In any case, both terms—"Christ" and "Messiah"—are titles by the time of the New Testament. They appear with the definite article: *the* Christ and *the* Messiah. And they appear in sentences like, "You are the Christ." Both the Greek and the Hebrew terms come from the word meaning "to anoint" in their respective languages. As noted earlier, they make sense only in a Jewish scriptural environment where anointing with oil was a ceremony of installation to office for kings and priests. For ordinary Greeks, "the Christos" would mean someone who had been smeared with oil, devoid of religious significance.

The use of the term "the Christ" presumes likewise a history of interpreting the Old Testament. While there are passages that speak of people who have been anointed, the particular grammatical form—the participle with the definite article "the"—does not appear in Israel's Bible. There is no *"the* Christ" in the Old Testament. The singling out of one figure who can be identified by Peter and the chief priest and the mockers occurred over a period of time. We have only limited access to that history of interpretation, though perhaps enough to understand the basic development. By studying literature from the period roughly between 200 BCE and 200 CE, we can get some sense of how a new understanding of some crucial biblical passages took shape. Books in the so-called Apocrypha, the Pseudepigrapha, the Dead Sea Scrolls, and the writings of the early rabbis provide the little evidence we possess.

An example of the development would be Psalm 2. The psalm speaks of a conspiracy against "the LORD and his anointed" (Ps 2:1-3). "His anointed" here refers to a king: "I have set my king on Zion, my holy hill," says the Lord God (2:6). This anointed King now speaks:

> I will tell of the decree of the LORD:
> He said to me, "You are my son;
>   today I have begotten you.
> Ask of me, and I will make the nations your heritage,
>   and the ends of the earth your possession.
> You shall break them with a rod of iron,
>   and dash them in pieces like a potter's vessel." (Ps 2:7-9)

Old Testament scholars attempt to locate the psalm in a setting that would explain its particular features. Most regard it as a

"Royal Psalm," seeing it perhaps as part of a service of installation for kings. By the first century, the psalm is understood as an oracle that speaks not about any king but about *the* King whom God will anoint at the end of days. Biblical passages that may have meant one thing in their historical setting have become part of visions and dreams of the future. Writings like the Psalms of Solomon and the Dead Sea Scrolls and the New Testament can presume such an interpretation without having to offer elaborate arguments to justify their reading. The author of the Letter to the Hebrews can presume his readers understand that this passage refers to a singular figure. He also presumes that the promise to David of an offspring who will sit on his throne refers to the same figure:

> When your days are fulfilled and you lie down with your ancestors, I will raise up your offspring after you, who shall come forth from your body, and I will establish his kingdom. He shall build a house for my name, and I will establish the throne of his kingdom forever. I will be a father to him, and he shall be a son to me.
>
> (2 Sam 7:12-14)

The author of Hebrews (1:5) knows that the "son" in 2 Samuel 7 is the same as the "son" in Psalm 2:7. Both speak of a king who will arise at the end of days. The same interpretation is presumed by a particular fragment among the Dead Sea Scrolls, known as 4QFlorilegium, which is dated prior to the Christian era. Such interpreters of Israel's scriptures were obviously not interested in locating the meaning of passages in their original historical setting. The "rules" of such scriptural interpretation are different enough from our own historical reading that it merits extensive study as a separate topic.[1]

Relevant for our purposes is the knowledge that the language of Mark's Gospel is not unique but presumes a whole history of interpreting Israel's scriptures. That "the Christ" does not need to be explained presumes that readers of the Gospel know what it means—knowledge that we can unearth by reading other works from Mark's historical and literary environment.[2] Because the topic has been discussed extensively elsewhere, a summary of relevant information is probably sufficient here.

1. When the term "Messiah" or "Christ" is used in the form with a definite article, whether in early Christian or Jewish litera-

ture, it refers to a royal figure—the King to come. That is what we find in Mark. There is ample evidence to indicate that in the first century CE (and perhaps first century BCE), those who heard the expression "the Messiah" would think of a King— with few exceptions, the king from the line of David who would arise at the end of days to save Israel.

2. While there is no uniformity even among traditions about this king, there is a constellation of biblical passages that appear with sufficient regularity so as to be viewed as constants, including Psalms 2, 89, and 132; 2 Samuel 7 (and parallels); Numbers 24:17; Genesis 49:10; Isaiah 11:1; and Jeremiah 23:5-6 and 33:17-22. The variety within visions of a messianic future is limited by the imagery appropriate to a king.

3. As a royal figure, "the Messiah" must be distinguished from other deliverers who appear in visions and dreams of the future. The view of the people that Jesus is "Elijah" or "one of the prophets" arises from other expectations, like the return of Elijah (Mal 4:5-6) or of the "prophet like Moses" (Deut 18:16-20). The small community of Jews living at Qumran on the shores of the Dead Sea whose views are represented in the Dead Sea Scrolls expected the coming of a priestly figure as well (Jer 33:17-18; Zech 6:12-13). While some of the traits could be exchanged, there was no general collapsing of one figure into another. Only later could Christian interpreters combine all the traits into one figure, culminating with Calvin's threefold office of prophet, priest, and king. The Dead Sea Scrolls offer a striking example of a vision of the future in which at least two deliverers are expected, both of whom are "anointed."[3]

4. While there is considerable debate about how central "the Messiah" was to Jewish visions and dreams of the future, there can be little doubt that the importance and centrality of royal ideology has been exaggerated and the variety within Jewish tradition underestimated. Not all Jews expected the coming of a King. For some, it was enough that God would preside at a final judgment.

5. There is no evidence that Jews believed the Messiah would suffer and die. In fact, there is every reason to believe that Jesus' suffering and death would have disqualified him as a candidate for royal office. Mark's portrayal of religious and

political expectations is accurate. Both the religious and political leaders think it absurd for anyone to claim that Jesus is the Messiah-King. That Jesus is the Christ comes as a surprise to everyone. What it means that he is the Christ involves rethinking the tradition. That is surely how we are to understand Paul's references to "Christ crucified" as "a stumbling block to Jews and foolishness to Gentiles" as well as "Christ the power of God and the wisdom of God" for those who have been called to faith (1 Cor 1:23-24).

The interesting result of such study is a sense that Jesus' question "Who do people say that I am?" could be answered in a variety of ways from within Jewish tradition, and that the opinion that Jesus was a prophet makes good sense. That he is a "King" makes little sense in light of traditional expectations. Jesus did little that was royal. And the point in the story when he is most consistently depicted with royal categories is the account of his trial and death—when he looks least like the coming royal deliverer.

Such observations help to underscore what we may already have observed in Mark. The Gospel does not in any way play down the apparent inappropriateness of the title "the Christ" for Jesus. The observations may also be of help in formulating some guesses about the historical events that led to Jesus' death—and why Jesus' followers confessed him as the Christ in the first place (see below).

"The Son of Man" (or "the son of man")

In older books on "the titles of Jesus," space is usually devoted to "the Son of Man." The peculiar expression has no known antecedent in Greek literature and its history is limited almost exclusively to the New Testament. It is not used by later Christian writers. That the expression is problematic ought to be apparent in the difficulty English translators have in deciding how to render it. The NRSV has "the Son of Man."

While not typical of scholarship, *The Living Bible* provides a glimpse of all the possibilities. In several instances, the translator renders the Greek as "the Messiah." He obviously regards "the Son of Man" as a title that refers to the Messiah: "I, the Messiah, have the authority on earth to forgive sins" (2:10). In other instances, he takes the Greek simply as a self-reference: "Then he began to tell them about the terrible thing *he* would suffer" (8:31 TLB, emphasis added). In one passage it is both a self-reference and a messianic title:

> And anyone who is ashamed of me and my message in these days of unbelief and sin, I, the Messiah, will be ashamed of him when I return in the glory of my Father, with the holy angels. (8:38 TLB)

Several book-length studies have been written on the enigmatic Greek expression, without achieving a consensus. For readers of Mark, knowledge of the thought world will not settle how to read the strange Greek expression. Perhaps the most important clues are within the narrative.

1. Only Jesus uses the expression, and he uses it as a self-reference. While there are some passages that might suggest he is speaking about someone else (8:38), there is no instance when a character in the story understands Jesus to be speaking of anyone but himself.
2. Matthew and Mark use "I" and "Son of Man" interchangeably. For Mark's "Who do people say that I am," Matthew reads, "Who do people say the Son of Man is"; for Mark's "And he began to teach them that the Son of Man must suffer many things" (8:31), Matthew reads, "He began to teach them how much he must suffer." The terms are interchangeable in the Gospels.
3. There is no instance in Mark where "the Son of Man" appears as a predicate in a sentence, like "Jesus is the Son of Man." It is difficult to understand it as a title without such an occurrence. Only usage outside the New Testament could justify such a reading, and the evidence is hardly convincing.
4. Some of the passages in which Jesus refers to himself in this unusual fashion include imagery from Daniel 7:9-14. The vision in which Daniel sees "one like a human being [lit., "like a son of man"] coming with the clouds of heaven" is somehow related to the expression. The phrase in Daniel, however, is a simile ("like") and does not account for the singular grammatical construction of the New Testament expression (lit., *the* Son of *the* Man).

There is a variety of explanations offered for the use of the strange expression. One is that the Greek translates literally an idiom in Aramaic—the language Jesus spoke—by which one could refer to oneself in the third person. The problem arises because Greek does not use the same idiom, and the expression does not really make sense in Greek. This would then explain why only Jesus uses the phrase in the Gospels: the tradition of Jesus' sayings tried to be faithful, even to the point of translating an idiom that does not work in Greek.

Scholars will continue to debate this question, and until more literature becomes available, it is unlikely the matter will be settled to anyone's satisfaction. For readers of Mark, it means that the best course is to work within the context of the narrative—recognizing, however, that translations will continue to interpret "son of man" in a variety of ways. We will probably do best to regard "the son of man" as a strange way Jesus referred to himself and not as a title referring to a heavenly deliverer. If there is a connection with the passage in Daniel, the context in Mark will usually make that clear.

CHAPTER 5

PLUNDERING SATAN'S HOUSE

The opening story in Jesus' public ministry is an exorcism. Jesus casts out an "unclean spirit" from a man in a synagogue on the sabbath (1:21-28). Comparison with the other Gospels only indicates how singular this beginning is. In Matthew, the first event in Jesus' public ministry narrated at length is a three-chapter "sermon" in which Jesus sketches what it means to be a disciple (Matthew 5–7). In Luke, the first event is a kind of inaugural address that occurs in Jesus' hometown. His reading of Isaiah and announcement that "this scripture is fulfilled in your hearing" attracts the attention of his audience. By the time he has finished speaking, they are ready to throw him off a cliff. In John, Jesus' first "sign" is transforming 120 gallons of water into wine at a wedding banquet. The exorcism in Mark introduces readers to a story with a distinctive cast.

Several things about the story in Mark are striking. First, the unclean spirit knows who Jesus is and is appropriately fearful:

What have you to do with us, Jesus of Nazareth? Have you come to destroy us? I know who you are, the Holy One of God. (1:24)

Supernatural beings know Jesus' identity, and as readers we are privy to the disclosures that come from heavenly voices and shrieking demoniacs (3:11; 5:7). Second is Jesus' authority: he commands ("rebukes") the demons, and they obey. Third is the effect on the crowds: they are stunned, frightened, impressed by his authority. These are not the only reactions, but they are typical.

Closely associated with Jesus' exorcisms are his healings. By the end of the first chapter, he has cast out a demon, cured Peter's mother-in-law, helped countless sick and possessed (1:35-38), and cleansed a leper. While Matthew emphasizes Jesus' teaching, in Mark Jesus is a man of action. He is a healer and exorcist. Not surprisingly, the Gospel contains numerous accounts of Jesus' dealings with the sick. Also not surprisingly, the followers he chooses to share his ministry are commissioned to preach and cast out demons (3:13-15) and also heal the sick (6:12-13).

The theme of Jesus' preaching, of course, is that the "kingdom of God is at hand" (1:15). The lack of detail may suggest that readers can be presumed to understand the Greek phrase variously rendered as "kingdom of God" or "rule of God." It is likewise the case that understanding the expression depends upon reading on in the story, where Jesus will speak of the kingdom of God by the use of analogies (parables). How the dawning of the Kingdom and Jesus' exorcisms are related is hinted at in a short but revealing passage midway through chapter three. Jesus speaks about "kingdoms" and "households" in response to the evaluation of religious authorities who attribute Jesus' powers to an alliance with the devil:

> And the scribes who came down from Jerusalem said, "He has Beelzebul, and by the ruler of the demons he casts out demons."
> (Mark 3:22)

Jesus responds:

> How can Satan cast out Satan? If a kingdom is divided against itself, that kingdom cannot stand. And if a house is divided against itself, that house will not be able to stand. And if Satan has risen up against himself and is divided, he cannot stand, but his end has come. But no one can enter a strong man's house and plunder his

property without first tying up the strong man; then indeed the
house can be plundered. (3:23-27)

The religious leaders who have come from Jerusalem cannot
deny Jesus' power. They attribute it to spirit possession, and they
are partly correct. But they do not recognize that Jesus is possessed by the Spirit of God ("he saw the Spirit coming down like
a dove into him" [1:10])—so their accusation constitutes "blasphemy against the Holy Spirit" (3:28-30).

On one level, Jesus' comments give voice to common sense: if
his healings and exorcisms are the result of demonic possession,
the scribes should rejoice, since Satan would be warring against
his own forces. The important point is that people are being set
free. The imagery of "kingdoms" and "households" is more suggestive, however. It offers a sense of how the Greek *basileia* is to
be understood: it envisions not only "ruling" but the actual space
of that rule. The image of the "house" will appear again in Mark.
Perhaps the most interesting occurrence is at the end of Jesus'
instructions about the future, which conclude with an analogy
about the lord of a house leaving his slaves in charge (13:33-37).
The world here is compared to a household in which someone is
in charge. Jesus' parable suggests that the devil is in control and
that the dawning of God's rule will mean dispossessing Satan.
The imagery is more developed in Luke's Gospel, where the devil
offers Jesus "all the kingdoms of the world...their glory and all
this authority; for it has been given over to me, and I give it to
anyone I please" (Luke 4:5-6). The most extreme form of the
notion appears in John's Apocalypse, where human government
is the embodiment of evil.

The imagery is not developed in Mark, and there is no reason
to presume a full-blown mythology behind the narrative. In a
simpler way, however, the metaphors do help make sense of the
story. If the drama in which the Spirit-empowered Jesus is
involved is the reclaiming of God's authority, and if that is what
the dawning of the kingdom of God means, Jesus is not simply the
herald but the agent. There can be little wonder that unclean
spirits fear Jesus' approach. It means their end is near. And it will
not be surprising that Jesus encounters trouble from the religious
and political leaders whose task is to preserve the kingdom of
Caesar and the house(hold) of God.

DEFEATING THE LEGION (5:1-20)

The account of Jesus' exorcism in the land of the Gerasenes is one of the longest stories in the synoptic Gospels. Matthew's and Luke's abbreviated versions make the same point but they do not have the same effect. The differences are most apparent when the stories are read aloud. Mark's love of detail stands out. The narrator speaks not only of "chains" used to restrain the hapless man but "chains" and "shackles":

> And no one could restrain him any more, even with a chain; for he had often been restrained with shackles [i.e., for the feet] and chains [for the hands], but the chains he wrenched apart, and the shackles he broke in pieces; and no one had the strength to subdue him. (5:3-4)

Some take the detail as a mark of authenticity. More helpful is to recognize how well the detail works in oral performance. It adds to an appreciation of the story, whose goal is to make it possible for an audience to experience the spectacle and not simply to report that it occurred. One mark of a good storyteller is attention to the details.

Other features of the story stand out. One is the imagery of ritual impurity, particularly important for those whose world is defined by the scriptures of Israel and the Law of Moses. Even those insensitive to such matters have learned that the spirits Jesus confronts are "unclean." In this story, everything suggests a setting that is ritually unclean, impure, out of bounds in view of the Law of Moses. The territory is obviously Gentile, since pigs—unclean animals—are present. The man with the "unclean spirit" lives among the tombs, likewise a place of impurity. If the man with the superhuman strength were not menacing enough, the setting exudes impurity and thus danger. Laws about ritual purity are designed to protect people. Jesus pays them no heed but intrudes into territory that is in every respect out of bounds, to confront a man who is beyond control and help.

As menacing as he seems, the demoniac is not an obvious threat to others. He is self-abusive ("howling and bruising himself with stones" [5:5]). The inability of the townspeople to control his behavior and his superhuman strength provide evidence that he is possessed. In their view, it is appropriate that he live among

110

the dead, outside the circle of civilized life. Another mark of his uncivilized behavior is his lack of clothing, about which we learn in retrospect (5:15).

A distinctive feature of the story is the lengthy exchange between Jesus and the demon. In most cases, the "confession" of the demon is followed by a rebuke and a command, and the exorcism is completed (1:23-27; 1:34; 9:25-26). The dialogue in this story is worth some attention. It is clear, first of all, that when the demoniac addresses Jesus, the one in charge—the one who speaks—is not the man but the unclean spirit who possesses him. The story is thus not a faith story about how someone asked Jesus for help and was rewarded. The man has no control. It is the demon—or, as we learn, demons—who are in charge.

The account is interested in names. The unclean spirit knows Jesus' name: he is "Jesus, Son of the Most High God." That the man bows before Jesus is an acknowledgment of his position and power. There is almost a touch of humor in the demon's attempt to invoke God's help in protecting him against Jesus ("I adjure you by God, do not torment me"), since Jesus is God's Son.

The name of the spirit is even more interesting. That a name is important is common to many cultures. Particularly in exorcisms, learning the demon's name is half the battle. The same interest is reflected in modern medicine: giving a malady a name is an essential part of the healing process. It is probably significant that in this story, Jesus learns the name from the spirit: "My name is Legion; for we are many" (5:9). The statement should probably be heard as a boast—an unfortunate one, since once Jesus knows the name he has power over the spirit. That seems to be presumed in the story, for after disclosing his name, the spirit—Legion—immediately begins to negotiate terms. The word *legion* is itself important. It is a Latin word, not Greek, and is associated with Roman military forces. More than one commentator has suggested that the story is really political, making veiled promises about deliverance from Roman oppression to people who lived under Roman occupation.[1] While not impossible, the association of the demon's name with military might works well within the story world. It explains why people had difficulty with the demoniac: he is possessed by a whole army!

Following the military metaphor, the Legion upon surrender must now sue for terms. The demons know they will be deprived of their lodging, since Jesus has commanded it. Where will Legion go? "Send us into the pigs." This should amuse readers, since we are expected to know that pigs are unclean animals. The unclean spirits do not wish to leave the region. They like the area—unclean land around the tombs—and would be at home in pigs. Jesus grants their request. Yet no sooner do they enter the pigs than the whole herd rushes into the water—thus "cleansing" the unclean spirits. That unclean spirits cannot tolerate water is a familiar motif in folklore, as anyone who has seen the *Wizard of Oz* knows. It is water that destroys the wicked witch. In Mark's story, it is water that destroys the unclean spirits. In a delightful tour de force, the spirits themselves choose the means of their own destruction—delightful, of course, to those who share the biblical notion that pigs are unclean animals. The story "delights" in the course of "teaching" and "moving" the audience.

The story takes on an ominous tone when the townspeople come to see what has occurred. While most contemporary readers are scandalized by the enormous loss of property, the townspeople are most impressed by the sight of the domesticated demoniac, "sitting there, clothed and in his right mind" (5:15). The narrator says simply, "and they were afraid." They react first to the power evident in the stranger. It does not say they were scandalized by the magnitude of their financial loss. Such sentiments are typical of our own culture and its preoccupation with private property. The villagers do not demand restitution or threaten to have Jesus arrested. They encourage him to leave. Their world has been invaded, and the prospects make them fearful. While they could not control the unclean spirits, they could at least get on with their lives as long as the possessed man lived apart, out of sight and hearing. Now one has come with the power to bind the strong man and plunder his house. For the demoniac that invasion has meant deliverance. The townspeople are unsure. Jesus threatens the stability of their carefully structured world, as he has for those whose everyday life is defined by the Law of Moses. And so they urge him to leave. The requests will become more urgent as the story progresses, until finally authorities take matters into their own hands and dispose of Jesus by force. If the deliverance of the demoniac in the land of the Gerasenes has proved costly to the townspeople, in the end Jesus will have to pay far more.

In a striking reversal, in response to the liberated demoniac's request to accompany Jesus, Jesus tells him, "Go home to your friends, and tell them how much the Lord has done for you, and what mercy he has shown you" (5:19). He is not commanded to keep quiet but to speak. And he does, throughout the Decapolis. When a Gentile woman comes to Jesus ("Greek, of Syrophoenician origin" [7:26]) with a request for help, we are perhaps to imagine that the word of the solitary Gentile evangelist has reached her.

It is most interesting to observe how the story of Jesus and the Gerasene demoniac works when it is performed. The reactions of an audience are culturally determined, and that is perhaps clearer here than in many other places. "Why did Jesus have to destroy all that property?" is a regular response. Not surprisingly, the comment comes from people whose world is defined by economic metaphors. Others may be more sympathetic to the pigs. The animal rights movement has had an impact on the culture as well. Very few pay any attention to the demoniac who is liberated from so impossible a bondage. The cost of his deliverance seems too high. Jesus should have found a more cost-effective way to perform the healing. The imagery of cost and payment provides an intriguing way into the rest of the Gospel story, since in the end Jesus' ministry will cost him everything.

Equally noteworthy is the reaction of young people who do not find the notion of unclean spirits at all foreign. While older readers often feel more comfortable with "scientific" explanations of the demoniac's behavior that offer a diagnosis by assigning the malady a different "name" like "schizophrenia," young people raised on films that depict demonic possession react with genuine interest in the supernatural dimensions of the story. In this regard they are more like members of other cultures whose world is alive with spirits, both good and evil. The uneasiness one can observe among the more scientifically minded is akin to the dis-ease experienced by the townspeople in the story. We inhabit worlds that are narrowly defined and bounded, and we are obliged to protect them against intruders. That is as true of our ideas and theories about illness and disease as it is of our homes and possessions.

The argument of this story is that Jesus is an intruder—and that unless he makes incursions into foreign territory, there is no hope of rescue. The story is told in vivid fashion to make possible an experience of Jesus' power, which is as dangerous as it is promising.

FREEING TWO WOMEN

Jesus' ministry of delivering people from Satan's hold is closely related to his ministry of healing. Illness was not understood in secular "scientific" terms as is typically the case in modern culture. Sickness had spiritual dimensions. Various types of disorders were directly ascribed to possession (Mark 9:17-29). Others could be understood as punishment for transgressions. As the disciples pass a blind man, they ask, "Who sinned, this man or his parents, that he was thus born blind?" (John 9:1-2). In 1 Corinthians 11:30, Paul suggests that eating the Lord's Supper unworthily has resulted in illness within the congregation. In Jesus' healing of the paralytic, he first forgives his sins, then instructs him to "stand up, take your mat and go to your home" (Mark 2:9-11). While no systematic theory holds all these notions together neatly, illness had spiritual dimensions and was related to sin and evil.

Two of the most dramatic healing stories occur in the same chapter as the exorcism of the Legion in the land of the Gerasenes. The stories—one about a woman suffering from a twelve-year-long hemorrhage and the other about a twelve-year-old girl at the point of death—are intertwined and must be read together. The "bracketing" of one story with another is familiar from elsewhere in the Gospel. In this case the point is simply to appreciate how the stories play off against one another.

The first person to whom we are introduced as Jesus arrives on the "other side" of the lake is a father who has come to plead for his daughter. The identification of the father, both by name and office, is unusual. He is singled out among those whom Jesus helps, perhaps because he is an official ("one of the leaders of the synagogue"). His position is understood within religious as well as social categories. He is one of the first "officials" from within the religious community to take any interest in Jesus. Perhaps this will be an important turning point in Jesus' ministry. The man is desperate, since his daughter is "at the point of death" (5:23). If Jesus is to help, he must hurry.

114

The desperate plight of a young child provides the setting for an interruption. The second person to whom we are introduced is given no name and has no office. She is described in a remarkable string of participles in Greek as no less desperate. She has been bleeding for twelve years. We are not given the details of her hemorrhage. We are told only how her efforts to secure help from the medical establishment have succeeded only in bankrupting her. The comment about physicians offers a sense of the social location of the narrator, who writes from below rather than above. Physicians, he suggests, take people's money and don't really help much.

The woman's strange behavior makes sense to anyone who knows the Law of Moses. The hemorrhage has rendered her unclean. She cannot participate in religious activity; anyone she touches will likewise become unclean. The woman is the starkest possible contrast to Jairus, a male and synagogue official. In addition to her lower status as a woman, she is suffering from a social disease as well as a physical malady and cannot even enter the synagogue. Thus she cannot identify herself to Jesus and ask for help—she would be driven off if discovered—but must try to conceal her problem if she is to get close enough to touch him. Her desperate faith is rewarded. The touch of Jesus' clothing is enough to heal her, as "power goes forth from him." Jesus is not defiled by her touch; she is cleansed. That Jesus makes a spectacle of her and praises her faith allows an opportunity to speak indirectly to the implied audience of the Gospel. The translation, "your faith has made you well" (5:34), might better be translated literally, "your faith has saved you." "Wellness" here includes more than a healthy body. It includes restoration to the human family and the ability to participate in the life of the synagogue.

Jesus' words to the woman are still reverberating as people come from "the leader's house" to report that the delay has proved fatal to the young girl. "Your daughter is dead. Why trouble the teacher any further?" (5:35). The impact is most clearly felt when the story is read aloud. Listening to the story in church, a young girl turned to her mother and said impatiently, in a stage whisper, "What about the little girl?" She knew exactly how the story worked. She experienced the disappointment of the announcement. Because he had taken time with the woman, a child had died. She also discovered that the anticlimax is only temporary, providing the occasion for an even more spectacular miracle. "Do not fear, only believe," Jesus tells Jairus, and they set out for his house with only the inner circle of the disciples as witnesses.

Mark relishes the detail in the story. The "commotion" at the house is caused by the professional mourners who have come, appropriately, to begin the lamentation that was part of the grieving process. They serve as "experts" on death. When Jesus insists the girl is only "sleeping," they act on behalf of all those who know the reality and finality of death. They laugh at him. Their disbelief further heightens the drama as Jesus and the small group go into the room alone with the young girl. The group stands outside, waiting to mock one who imagines death to be no more than sleep.

Reminiscent of stories told about Elijah and Elisha, Jesus brings the young girl back to life. His words, "Talitha cum," are given in Aramaic. They are translated ("which means, 'Little girl, get up'") to avoid misunderstanding them as magic words, but the foreign language gives the story a particular effect. There is something mysterious about the words, and their mere presence suggests some distance from Jesus—who did, in fact, speak another language. Readers experience some sense of distance from the events while at the same time experiencing the power of the story. Once again, the Aramaic words have the greatest impact when the story is read aloud.

When the little girl arises, Jesus tells the parents to give her something to eat. The point is perhaps the same as in Luke 24:36-43, where the risen Jesus' eating in the presence of the disciples, is part of his proof that he is not a "ghost."

The one strange feature in the story is Jesus' command that those present in the room tell no one: "He strictly ordered them that no one should know this" (5:43). The whole story has been moving toward a dramatic triumph at the end, as Jesus leads the young girl out in view of the mourners who have just laughed at him. One would expect some statement of their amazement and perhaps a comment that his fame spread throughout the countryside, as is the case in Matthew 9:18-26. At one level the command does not make sense. We can hardly imagine that the matter can be kept a secret or the young girl hidden. Readers might be tempted to extract more from the injunction than can be justified—a regular practice among commentators. That might be justifiable if it were not for the recurrence of this theme throughout the story. Jesus' command to keep silent about healings and about his identity is a regular feature of the story (see below on "Secrets and Secrecy").

While an explanation of the strange injunction to keep silent must be sought within the story, the distinction between "story" and "discourse" is helpful. While confusing at the level of the story, the conclusion makes sense as intended for the reader. We have a sense of how the story should end, with a kind of closure and satisfaction at Jesus' having silenced his critics and brought the victory over death into the light of day. There is no such satisfaction at the end of this story. The command to remain silent short-circuits the process. Such an observation may contribute to an interpretation of the ending. It is, after all, part of a larger story that will have just as unsatisfying a conclusion, except that when the women are finally instructed to tell, they remain silent (16:8). Understanding how these inconclusive endings work on readers will surely be high on the interpretative agenda.

The two stories are meant to be enjoyed. The interplay of social class differences, religious notions of ritual purity, the interruption, false climaxes and building toward a final climax—these are features of a story that intends to delight and move an audience. While we may understand what these stories "mean," that is not a sufficient way to appreciate them.

WHERE THE DEVIL DID THE DEVIL GO?

The prominence of exorcisms in the public ministry of Jesus raises a major question for the second half of the story: What happens to Satan and the unclean spirits? With Jesus' exorcism of the young man immediately following the Transfiguration (9:14-27), nothing more is said of Satan. In Luke's Gospel, at least, there is some transition: Satan, who has been waiting for an "opportune time" since Jesus' temptation (Luke 4:13), "enters Judas," initiating the events that will lead to Jesus' death (Luke 22:3). Authority, both religious and political, apparently belongs to Satan's dominion (Luke 4:6). Mark makes no such transition, and we are left to imagine the relationship between Jesus' plundering of Satan's stronghold and the ensuing events that will lead to his death.

That there is a significant interpretive problem here has been recognized for some time. Albert Schweitzer pointed to the abrupt shift in the story when Jesus announces that he will go to Jerusalem. He spoke of the shift from Jesus' nonmessianic ministry to his messianic death.[2] Jesus' activities of teaching, healing, and exorcising do not belong to traditions about the coming Messiah-King. Teaching and healing are the sorts of things expected of a prophet like Elijah or Moses, both of whom were expected to play a role in the age to come (Deut 18:16-20 and Malachi 4:5-6 were passages Jesus' contemporaries believed pointed to the great days toward which history was moving). How does Jesus' "royal office" relate to the previous phase in his career?

The Gospel writer offers no explicit help for interpreters. Perhaps it is because he did not himself understand (Schweitzer's explanation). Or it may be that we are to see the confrontation with the religious and political authorities as the climax of God's dealing with the domain of the devil. Framing questions here will be important. Selecting either Jesus' conflict with Satan or his conflict with the religious authorities as the major theme in the story is illegitimate. Both are present. Lacking explicit warrant, we must venture a guess about how the author understood the relationship between the forces of the devil and the political and religious authorities. Later tradition unified the two themes. Such an understanding is probably implied in Mark.

Perhaps we may understand the conflict so central to the story in terms of bondage. Those who are possessed by Satan are not in control and are thus unable to free themselves. The sick are likewise bound by some malady. Even the allegedly free and healthy turn out to be in bondage, however. Peter's problem, we learn, is that his mind is set on human things rather than on God's things (8:33). Is it any different for the religious leaders? The Gospel gives no reason to trust that the legitimate authorities—the Temple protectors and the guardians of law and order—understand better than anyone else what is the case. They cannot appreciate the contrast between "God's ways" and "human ways." They seem blind and deaf to the truth; their hearts have apparently been hardened. In that sense their plight is little different from that of the demoniacs and the sick whom Jesus healed. They are bound, blind and deaf. If there is any hope for them, it will have to come from outside themselves.

CHAPTER 6

THE
TEACHER

The question, Martin Dibelius once suggested, is not why Mark includes so little of Jesus' teaching (in comparison with Matthew and Luke) but why he includes any at all. In Mark's Gospel, we have observed, Jesus is a man of action. He heals, casts out demons, feeds multitudes with a few loaves. He has come to "plunder the strong man's house." Yet the story makes repeated reference to Jesus' teaching. In fact, the verb "to teach" and the nouns "teaching" and "teacher" occur more frequently in Mark than in Matthew or Luke. While Jesus is thus far more than a sage, his teaching—reported in several blocks—is an important aspect of his career.

"IN PARABLES"

While Jesus' controversies with the Pharisees about how to understand the Law include pithy sayings, the first sustained example of Jesus' teaching is the little collection of parables in chapter four. To be accurate, the collection includes some isolated sayings (4:21-25) along with three extended analogies drawn from agricultural life. The simple stories have spawned an enormous literature, suggesting that the stories are perhaps not as simple as they appear.

Behind the Story

Interpreting the parables is one place where the various strategies of reading become particularly clear. The approach that has dominated scholarship almost since the turn of the century is historical. In the Middle Ages Jesus' parables were read as allegories with almost limitless applications. In this century most interpreters have consciously departed from allegory. What has driven the scholarly study of parables is the conviction that the parables should be read in their original historical setting. What they "mean" is what they "meant" to the original author and audience. Because most scholars have been convinced that Jesus actually spoke in parables, "original author" here refers to Jesus. The task of interpretation, therefore, is to get at "what Jesus meant." This assumes there is a correct reading of a parable and that it is to be found in Jesus' intention.[1]

If that is the agreed-upon goal of interpretation, a problem is that we cannot necessarily trust that the Gospels have provided us with Jesus' exact words and the situation in which the parables were actually spoken. There are reasons for suspicion. The most obvious problem is that Jesus spoke Aramaic and the New Testament renders the parables in Greek. That there are differences among the Gospels in the wording of the parables is hardly surprising. Some of the differences may be due to translation. The parable in Matthew that compares the kingdom of heaven to a wedding banquet (Matt 22:1-10) is told in Luke as a story about a "great dinner" (Luke 14:15-24). The same Aramaic word can be translated as "wedding banquet" or "great dinner." There are other differences that are probably not the result of translation. In Matthew's story, the one who gives the banquet is a king; in Luke, it is simply a man. The tendency to elaborate and allegorize Jesus' stories is apparent from the first. The differences may not be great, but if the desire is to reconstruct what Jesus really said, choices must be made among the differences. The parable of the sower features some significant differences among the three versions in Matthew, Mark, and Luke.

A greater problem is the setting of the parables. The same parable may appear in a different place, with implications for what it means. Did Jesus intend the little story of the shepherd and the lost sheep as a response to disgruntled scribes and Pharisees (Luke 15:3-7), emphasizing joy in heaven over the repentance of a sinner, or as part of instructions to the disciples about how far they ought to go to bring back errant members who have strayed from the fold (Matt 18:12-14)? Perhaps Jesus intended both meanings and told this parable more than once. The problem of setting is obvious, however. It determines how the analogy is being used and what is being compared to what. If the church told Jesus' stories in new settings—as has always been the case—getting back to what Jesus originally intended will require some effort, since all we have are records of their usage. How the reconstructed "original" will be related to new contexts in the present will continue to pose challenges for preachers.

The parable of the sower, prominently featured in Mark 4, is told in both Matthew and Luke, with some significant differences. A synopsis, which prints the three Gospels in parallel columns, highlights the differences. How much detail did Jesus' parable of the sower contain? Luke's version is shortest and includes the fewest embellishments. In Luke, the disciples ask Jesus about "the parable" (Luke 8:9), rather than "the parables" (Mark 4:10). Jesus' explanation for speaking in parables is shortest in Luke (8:10), longer in Mark (4:11-12), and filled out by a lengthy citation from Isaiah in Matthew (13:13-15). Which were Jesus' words? Interpreters who insist on knowing what Jesus intended for his original audience must make decisions.

Complicating matters further is the version of the parable offered in the noncanonical *Gospel of Thomas*, a short book that records versions of Jesus' sayings that are not derived from the canonical Gospels but seem to represent an independent tradition. The parable of the sower is short and is given without the allegorical explanation familiar from Matthew, Mark, and Luke.

> Jesus said: Behold, the sower went out, he filled his hand, he sowed. Some fell on the road. The birds came and gathered them up. Others fell on the rock and did not send a root down into the earth, and did not send an ear up to heaven. And others fell upon

the good earth; and it brought forth good fruit up to heaven. It bore sixty-fold and one hundred and twenty-fold.[2]

What are we to make of the evidence? Scholars like Joachim Jeremias have argued that the data make sense if the Gospel writers inherited their material from an oral tradition in which the parables have undergone a transformation.[3] Moving back to the original means understanding how the changes took place. In the case of the parable of the sower, the first step is source analysis. The parable of the sower can easily be broken down into three parts: 4:3-9, 10-12, and 13-20. First is the parable, ending with, "Let anyone with ears to hear listen!" (4:3-9). Verse 10 presumes a change in setting:

When he was alone, those who were around him along with the twelve asked him about the parables.

Further, the question asked has to do with "the parables" (4:10). Jesus' explanation for choosing parables as his mode of discourse is not unrelated to the initial parable but its scope is far broader.

And he said to them, "To you has been given the secret of the kingdom of God, but for those outside, everything comes in parables; in order that

'they may indeed look, but not perceive,
and may indeed listen, but not understand;
so that they may not turn again and be forgiven.'"

He comments on the practice of speaking "in parables" before giving insiders an explanation. For source critics, the break is a sign that the explanation is not original to the parable. Verses 10-12 must thus be excluded from consideration.

Returning to an implied question about "this parable" (v. 13), Jesus offers an extended allegorical interpretation of the original parable in which the meaning of each feature is specified (vv. 13-20). Those interested in source analysis point out that there is some tension between the allegorical interpretation and the parable it seeks to interpret. While the original story is about a farmer who sows seed and the fate of four separate batches of seed, the allegorical interpretation is about reception. The problem is that the explanation does not work grammatically. The seed, we are told in the explanation, means "the word": "The sower sows the word" (4:14). Each of the following comments begins with a relative pronoun: "these are the ones" (vv. 15, 16, 18); "those" (v. 20 RSV). Their antecedents are four pronouns indicating batches of seed ("some" [v. 4], "other" [v. 5], "other" [v. 7], "other" [v. 8]). There is a good deal of awkwardness in the Greek. The relative pronouns in the allegorical explanation are masculine, while the originals are neuter. The allegory, in other words, reads the collective pronouns as references to "people." But while the original pronouns refer to batches of seed, in the allegory they cannot, since *seed* means "word." The four groups in the allegory are thus four different types of soil. Not without difficulty, the parable becomes an account of reception. In the statement "they immediately receive it with joy" (4:16), "they" must refer to the soil. While English translations smooth over some of the awkwardness, it is nevertheless apparent that the allegorical interpretation is purchased at some expense in terms of grammar and clarity.

One explanation for the awkwardness is that Jesus did not allegorize his parable; later interpreters did. While Jesus' story was about the sower and the fate of his seeding, the story becomes in later tradition an allegory about different kinds of soil. For one interested in Jesus' parable, the allegorical explanation would thus have to be stripped away and disregarded as well, leaving as the original parable verses 3-8. This is more likely the parable Jesus told. Interpreters who want to know what he originally meant must then reconstruct a situation in which he told it—to whom and for what reason.

It is unnecessary to proceed further down this road. If the task seems complicated, that is because it is complicated. Jeremias may well be correct about alterations in the parables and the new setting in which they have been placed. Working back through all the possible changes to the story Jesus told, however, and then reconstructing the precise setting in which it first appeared is not only complicated but surely beyond the abilities of all but a few scholars. Given the available evidence, the likelihood that the handful of experts will agree is slim. And even if there were some agreement and people were able to read Jesus' mind to know what he intended, the result would not be an interpretation of the Bible. Dissecting Mark's Gospel will not result in a reading of

Mark but of something else. For our purposes, such scholarship, while interesting, is secondary to the most pressing task. We are interested in Mark's Gospel and the place of the parables within that narrative setting.

Within the Story

THE PROMISE OF A HARVEST

The first thing to say about the parable of the sower is that it is read as an allegory in Mark. Jesus offers the authoritative reading. The parable is read as an account of the reception of seed (= the word) by various audiences. Preaching the word, which is what Jesus has been doing, will encounter obstacles. It already has. As readers we know more than Jesus' hearers can be expected to know. We are aware of the criticisms of the pious and their suspicions generated by Jesus' ministry among the sick and possessed. The parable speaks to the implied criticisms. Much effort would appear to be wasted. Seed is thrown with apparent careless abandon; loss is apparent everywhere. Satan snatches the word from some, preventing hearing and understanding; others have no depth; still others seem to offer promise, but the cares of the world choke off the seed and it is fruitless. One group—the good soil—receives the word and produces abundantly. That seems to make the whole enterprise worth the trouble. The farmer apparently knows his business after all. While the field does not look promising, there is reason to trust the one who sows the word with such abandon.

Connections with the story that follows seem obvious. The identification of Jesus as the Sower is natural. While the parable is not a neat plot summary, we will hear about those whom Satan prevents from hearing. At least one potential follower will go away grieving because he cannot give up his wealth (10:17-22). Perhaps most striking is the relationship between the disciples and the "rocky ground": when persecution comes, they will fall away (14:50). We may even wonder about the possible wordplay between the name of "Peter"—which means "Rock" *(petros)* and "Rocky Ground" *(petrodes)*. Peter will come closest to faithfulness, but his disintegration will be the worst. Under interrogation by servants, he will deny Jesus three times, with an oath (14:66-72).

124

But what about the concluding image in the parable? If Jesus' ministry will result in a great harvest, where and when will that be? The story Mark tells is one in which all his efforts seem to prove fruitless. In speaking of all the difficulties facing the sower, the parable speaks the truth. What of the promise of an abundant harvest?

The same question may be asked of the other two parables in Mark 4, the seed growing secretly (4:26-29) and the mustard seed (4:30-32). Each speaks of the kingdom of God in terms of a contrast between a time of humble beginnings and the time of harvest. In the second of the stories, the only significant activity is the sowing. The farmer plants and must then wait. Growth cannot be coerced or controlled. Those who plant must wait patiently for the results to appear. And they do. Without the effort of the farmer, the "earth produces of itself" (4:28). While it may take time, and while the results are frustratingly beyond the control of the farmer, the harvest will come.

The third parable contrasts the mustard seed with the plant it produces. This is what the kingdom of God is like. The humble beginnings in Jesus' ministry would seem to have little to do with the kingdom of God. But perhaps that ministry is related to the Kingdom as a seed is to the plant. The reality is there, at work, even if nothing is obvious and the seed seems so small. Once put into the ground, natural processes are a kind of guarantee. The result will be the largest of all shrubs, substantial enough for birds to nest in its shade (4:32).

In the context of Jesus' ministry that begins with an announcement that the kingdom of God is at hand, the parables offer an interpretation, anticipating objections. Jesus' ministry is the time of planting and humble beginnings. Obstacles seem overwhelming and the results unimpressive. In time, however, the harvest will come. Readers will want to know how to evaluate the parables. Do they speak the truth? The question cannot be answered apart from the story that follows.

INSIDE AND OUT

The second thing to note is that verses 10-12 locate the parable and explanation within the construct of inside and outside. Jesus' teaching in this chapter in fact heightens the contrast between insiders and outsiders. That such contrasts exist is not new. In fact, that seems to be one of the major functions of the third chapter. Jesus "creates" a group of twelve to be with him and to do what he does (3:13-19). They are contrasted with relatives (3:21), "your mother and your brothers and sisters" (3:32), and scribes (3:22)—all of whom believe Jesus is in one way or another not in control of himself. They are correct, but as outsiders they do not understand that it is the Spirit of God that drives Jesus.

Jesus' teaching distinguishes between insiders and outsiders. "To you has been given the mystery of the kingdom of God; to those outside everything is in parables [or riddles]." Jesus' disciples get explanations. The singling out of the disciples as insiders is emphasized a second time at the conclusion of Jesus' teaching (4:33-34). The Gospel does not explain what "the mystery of the kingdom of God" is. It does suggest that having that "secret" will be crucial:

> Pay attention to what you hear; the measure you give will be the measure you get, and still more will be given you. For to those who have, more will be given; and from those who have nothing, even what they have will be taken away. (4:24-25)

This special "something" will prove to be critical. Perhaps it will be the secret to growth and productivity. The chapter takes pains to identify the disciples as insiders and to suggest how important this is. In fact, nothing less than forgiveness seems to be at stake. In the most difficult saying in the whole Gospel, Jesus explains what it will mean to be an outsider:

> But for those outside, everything comes in parables; in order that they may indeed look, but not perceive, and may indeed listen, but not understand; so that they may not turn again and be forgiven.
> (4:11-12)

The concealment apparently will not last forever. "Nothing is hidden, except to come to light" (4:22). That Jesus conceals anything crucial, however, on which understanding depends and that will result in "turning" and forgiveness—even if just for a time—seems unfair. We shall take the matter up again. At least this much seems clear: the story invests a great deal in the disciples. If the parables truthfully depict how it will be with the kingdom of God, we may ask how they help us understand the story as it unfolds. The investment in the disciples would suggest they are the good soil. They at least will be productive. Selected by Jesus to share his ministry, they will be the ones who continue the task of planting that will result in the abundant harvest. The disciples' consistent lack of understanding, however, and their outright misunderstanding raise a critical question about Jesus' choice: Does he know what he is doing? Will Jesus' planting amount to anything at all? Once again, interpreting the parables must involve reading on in the story.

On This Side of the Story

Another sort of question leads in a very different direction. We may explore the meaning of the parables within the context of the narrative and how, for example, they are related to the career of the disciples. But how do they work on present readers? What do the parables do?

One of the things they may do is to awaken uneasiness. Perhaps the most common interpretation of the parable of the sower is that in its present form, it becomes an exhortation to "be good soil." Even that statement ought to give pause, however. "Be good soil" is at best an unfortunate choice of images. I recall the first class in which some students from rural communities asked about it. "How can soil be addressed to do something?" they asked. "Were the ancients so naive? Soil is something that is acted upon. It is disked and plowed and seeded and weeded and fertilized. But there are limits. Some soil is so poor that nothing can make it produce. If the point of the parable is to exhort people to produce, why use the image of dirt?" Why indeed!

What suggests that the parable is exhortation? The only imperative in the entire parable is the command "Listen!" The exhortations that follow the parable—to listen for that crucial thing without which "even what they have will be taken away"—do not help. How do people know what to listen for? And what if they cannot hear? The imagery in the parable is passive. Nothing suggests that the point of the story is that soil can change itself or cultivate itself or keep the birds away. The parable speaks about how things are. The only one in the whole chapter who seems to have any control at all is Jesus, who conceals crucial truths from those "outside."

The more one wrestles with the parable, the more difficult it becomes. It is true at the level of ordinary readers, and it is also the case with the most sophisticated. Verses 10-12 in particular have a way of attracting attention. Frank Kermode is aware of them, and his reading of Mark indicates that he finds the words both true and alienating.[4] He dedicates his study of secrecy in Mark "to those on the outside." Meir Sternberg, the fine student of Hebrew literature, finds these verses to be the most offensive in the Christian Bible.[5]

The parables portray a world in which the obstacles to understanding and productivity are legion. That may ring true. How can something as insignificant as "the word" change the face of reality? The parables speak about the kingdom of God in terms of promise, but they do not leave the fulfillment of that promise within the power of any human being—none within the story and certainly not readers. If there is to be a harvest, if anyone is to be productive, if any particular people are to be included in the harvest in the kingdom of God, it will be because they have been given a gift. And the only one who can give that gift is God. But will it be given? Is there any reason to believe that the seed will take root in any particular life, our own for example? Is there a reason to trust the God who is invested in the ministry of Jesus? It is difficult for most readers to say yes. What evidence is there? Jesus conceals the truth lest people turn and be forgiven. He apparently is not bound by notions of fairness.

In my experience as a teacher, the result of working at interpretation of the parable of the sower confirms Jesus' strategy. He tells parables, he says, to keep those outside from repenting. And that's generally the way it works. One of my students put it most forcefully: "I will not believe in a God who hardens!" she said through clenched teeth. Like most readers, she was hardened, as Jesus promised. The parable succeeded in keeping her outside. What will change things? It is not enough to point out that the stories are all about promises of harvest and celebration and safety. They are good news only if they are so for someone in particular. How can such stories be experienced as good news by readers on this side of the story? That the question is so seldom asked by commentators may suggest that the task of interpretation is an effort to avoid it, to divert attention to someone else, to another time and place. If the question is how Mark's Gospel works here, among us, there is nothing more important than getting an answer. Does the kingdom of God have anything to do with us in particular? Are we to be included in the harvest? The parables do not answer the questions. Interpreting the parables thus becomes part of interpreting the whole Gospel. We shall have to read on to discover what becomes of Jesus' planting and if there is reason to trust the God at whose mercy the parables seem to leave readers.

TAKING UP THE CROSS: INSTRUCTIONS ON FOLLOWING (8:31–10:45)

The second major block of teaching in Mark follows Peter's confession and Jesus' first announcement of his impending death (and resurrection). Peter's inability to hold together his confession of Jesus as "the Christ" and the course Jesus describes leads to an extended discussion of what it means to be a follower:

> He called the crowd with his disciples, and said to them, "If any want to become my followers, let them deny themselves and take up their cross and follow me. For those who want to save their life will lose it, and those who lose their life, for my sake and for the sake of the gospel, will save it. For what will it profit them to gain the whole world and forfeit their life?" (8:34-36)

The disciples have been called to be with Jesus and to share his ministry of preaching and healing (3:13-15). They have had some success in that ministry already (6:7-13). Beginning with Jesus' announcement of his coming confrontation, however, the matter of following focuses particularly on Jesus' death. The reference to "cross" at this point in the narrative makes sense only to those who know how the story turns out—that is, it makes sense only to readers who either know the story already or who are reading it for a second time.

Jesus' words seem a call to martyrdom. In what follows, however, it is not so much the prospect of death that is the focus. The issue seems more a matter of status. That is clearer in the case of Jesus' second prediction (9:31-32), which is followed by another inappropriate response from the disciples.

> And when he was in the house he asked them, "What were you arguing about on the way?" But they were silent, for on the way

they had argued with one another who was the greatest. He sat down, called the twelve, and said to them, "Whoever wants to be first must be last of all and servant of all." (9:33-35)

The issue of status is even more clearly developed in the disciples' response to the last of Jesus' predictions, the most complete and detailed (10:33-34).

James and John, the sons of Zebedee, came forward to him and said to him, "Teacher, we want you to do for us whatever we ask of you." And he said to them, "What is it you want me to do for you?" And they said to him, "Grant us to sit, one at your right hand and one at your left, in your glory." (10:35-37)

We must imagine either a throne scene or perhaps a banquet ("the kingdom of God is like a wedding feast") at which seats next to the King are places of honor. Jesus began his ministry with the announcement that the kingdom of God is at hand, and by this point in the story he has spoken of the Resurrection and of his glorious return more than once. The sons of Zebedee are thus not totally wrong in seeking to reserve seats when the harvest is in and the celebrating begun. They seem to understand something about the impending victory. They have no idea, however, what it will be like to be at Jesus' right and left hands. Those places will be reserved for bandits who hang with "the King of the Jews," one at his right and one at his left (15:27).

The other disciples respond indignantly to the request of James and John. They covet such places of honor for themselves.

So Jesus called them and said to them, "You know that among the Gentiles those whom they recognize as their rulers lord it over them, and their great ones are tyrants over them. But it is not so among you; but whoever wishes to become great among you must be your servant, and whoever wishes to be first among you must be slave of all. For the Son of Man came not to be served but to serve, and to give his life a ransom for many." (10:42-45)

The problem in the last two instances is not cowardice in the face of threatened martyrdom. "Taking up your cross" and "losing your life" are realities that have to do with the structure of community life and the organization of authority. Particularly in

130

the last of the three instances, it is clear that there will be some within the community who will exercise authority (see 13:34-36). The implied questions to which Jesus' teaching is a response have to do with such matters as self-promotion and status. Among the Gentiles, Jesus says, authority is something to be exercised "over" or "against" others. For those who follow Jesus, authority is something to be exercised on behalf of others. Greatness will be measured by the service one is able to render.

This issue of status among those who will follow Jesus explains the place of other material in this section of the Gospel that may seem out of place. There is, for example, a discussion of divorce (10:2-12), of the status of children (10:13-16), and of wealth and possessions (10:17-30). Each of these discussions has something to do with the shape of a community that follows the crucified one.

The first question asked Jesus is about divorce:

Some Pharisees came, and to test him they asked, "Is it lawful for a man to divorce his wife?" (10:2)

The question is not frivolous. The issue of the circumstances under which divorce was permitted was debated among the rabbis, as we noted earlier. In a society in which only the wealthiest of women in urban settings could own property, divorce meant being cut off from the ability to sustain life. Liberal divorce laws meant that women could be turned out, threatening them with poverty. The same is true in every society, though Western cultures tend to ignore the economic realities in favor of matters having to do with personal feelings.

According to Mark, Jesus did not side with the school of Shammai or the school of Hillel in this matter. Instead, he argued that God's intention is apparent in Genesis, where it speaks of two becoming one flesh. "What God has joined together, let no one put asunder." The passage in Deuteronomy is given only because of "your hardness of heart." His forbidding of divorce is clearly a statement about the status of women in society. They are to be safeguarded as vulnerable members of society.

That also explains the passage about Jesus and the children that follows (10:13-16). Women and children were both vulnerable members of society. Crucial to their survival has always been economic support. Easy divorce of women with young children means abrogating responsibility for caring for the most important members of society at a time of maximum vulnerability. The community that forms around Jesus will be an alternative community. "Mothers and brothers and sisters" will be linked not first of all by blood but by ideology. Their well-being, however, is crucial to everyone in the new family, particularly to those who have authority.

The need to provide support for the most vulnerable touches directly on economic realities. The story of Jesus' meeting with a rich man indicates that God's priority is caring for those in need—and that the lures of wealth and the temptation to ignore the poor are almost irresistible, as Jesus explained in his comments on the parable of the sower (4:19) and as he develops further here (10:24-31). They can choke even good seed that might be productive. There is hope for change only because with God all things are possible.

Such teachings have little impact on the disciples during the course of Jesus' ministry. They seem intended more clearly for the implied audience who know the story of Jesus' death on the cross and are in a position to reflect on what it will mean to follow.

A GLIMPSE OF THE FUTURE

"The Beginning of the Birth Pangs"

Chapter thirteen forms the last major block of instructional material. Jesus' discourse on what is to come follows directly the story of the widow who puts her last two coins into the Temple treasury. Far from offering a good example, the story of the poor widow gives an indication of why the Temple will be destroyed.

> As he taught, he said, "Beware of the scribes, who like to walk around in long robes, and to be greeted with respect in the marketplaces, and to have the best seats in the synagogues and places of honor at banquets! *They devour widows' houses* and for the sake of appearance say long prayers. They will receive the greater condemnation." (12:38-40, emphasis added)

It is the "scribes, chief priests, and elders," those responsible for the operation of Jerusalem and the Temple, who will condemn Jesus to death and hand him over to Pilate. Here, the scribes are castigated for living off the poor ("devouring widows' houses"). The story of the poor widow follows:

> He sat down opposite the treasury, and watched the crowd putting money into the treasury. Many rich people put in large sums. A poor widow came and put in two small copper coins, which are worth a penny. Then he called his disciples and said to them, "Truly I tell you, this poor widow has put in more than all those who are contributing to the treasury. For all of them have contributed out of their abundance; but she out of her poverty has put in everything she had, all she had to live on." (12:41-44)

The widow who puts in "all she had to live on" will be one of the last to be so used: "Not one stone will be left here upon another; all will be thrown down" (13:2).

Jesus' prediction of the Temple's destruction is no surprise. Earlier in the story he "cursed" the Temple as he cast out money changers (11:17), quoting a passage from Jeremiah's sermon against Solomon's Temple. The Temple has become corrupt and will be destroyed.

Many commentators believe that Mark's Gospel was written after the Jerusalem Temple was destroyed by the Romans in 70 CE. If not for the original audience, then certainly for all subsequent readers, Jesus' prophecy was fulfilled. The Temple was destroyed, never to be rebuilt. The reliability of Jesus' prophecies will be an important issue in making sense of the Gospel story as a whole, particularly of the ending.

The prospect of the Temple's destruction introduces the larger topic of Jesus' instructions:

> When he was sitting on the Mount of Olives, opposite the temple, Peter, James, John, and Andrew asked him privately, "Tell us, when will this be, and what will be the sign that all these things are about to be accomplished?" (13:3-4)

The questions elicit a lengthy response that is generally termed the "Markan Apocalypse." The designation is used on the one hand to mark the stylistic singularity of the chapter. It speaks exclusively about the future, sometimes using imagery drawn from Daniel that also appears in John's Apocalypse. Talk of the "desolating sacrilege" (13:14) and the "Son of Man coming in clouds" with great power and glory is reminiscent of the visionary material common to Daniel, the Enoch literature, 4 Ezra, and the Revelation of John.

The term is only modestly helpful, however, for Jesus' discourse is not "an apocalypse." It is a brief speech in a narrative. And even within the speech, most of the customary features of apocalyptic literature are missing. The bizarre visionary imagery is limited, as will become obvious to anyone who tries to work through the central chapters in the book of Revelation or Daniel. The forecast is more interested in the way the cosmic disruptions will affect the community of believers. There will be family divisions "because of my name" (13:12-13), something the behavior of Jesus' own family anticipates. There will be pretenders within the community of the faithful intent on "leading the elect astray" (13:6, 22). The specific instructions about fleeing Judea (13:14-20) may point to the aftermath of the war against Rome.

One of the major points of the instructions is that the various signs of trouble are not yet the end (13:7). They are only the beginning of the "birthpangs" (13:8). The image, employed by Paul in Romans 8:22, imagines the immediate future as a painful time that must precede the birth of a new age. Discipleship is lived out in the interim, prior to the end. Suffering in such a situation may actually produce hope if one can trust that there will be a good ending. This is what Jesus promises:

> Then they will see "the Son of Man coming in clouds" with great power and glory. Then he will send out the angels, and gather his elect from the four winds, from the ends of the earth to the ends of heaven. (13:26-27)

The discourse opened with the disciples' questions, "When will this be?" and "What will be the signs?" Having spoken about the signs, Jesus addresses the question of when:

> Truly I tell you, this generation will not pass away until all these things have taken place. Heaven and earth will pass away, but my words will not pass away. (13:30-31)

The promise is immediately qualified, however:

> But about that day or hour no one knows, neither the angels in heaven, nor the Son, but only the Father. (13:32)

The qualification points back to the warnings that "the end is still to come" (13:7) and, "This is but the beginning of the birthpangs" (13:8). What it means to live both with burning confidence in the nearness of the end and with uncertainty about the precise time is spelled out in the little parable with which Jesus ends the discourse.

"Stay Awake"

The story that provides a transition from Jesus' instructions to the account of his last hours offers a perspective on the impending future.

> Beware, keep alert; for you do not know when the time will come. It is like a man going on a journey, when he leaves home and puts his slaves in charge [lit., "gives his slaves authority"], each with his work, and commands the doorkeeper to be on the watch. Therefore, keep awake—for you do not know when the master of the house will come, in the evening, or at midnight, or at cockcrow, or at dawn, or else he may find you asleep when he comes suddenly. And what I say to you I say to all: Keep awake. (13:33-37)

One of the ways visionary literature has functioned is to give hope to the oppressed. At impossible times, they are encouraged to hold fast in view of the end, which is not far off and will provide vindication of the faithful. The little parable of Jesus does not imagine such a situation. It pictures the time before the end in terms of a house in which slaves are "in charge" (lit., "have authority"). They are not helpless but have both authority and assigned tasks. Most important is to watch for the return of the lord of the manor. The temptation will be to fall asleep. The parable does not say why it would be a bad thing to be caught asleep. Matthew's version of the parable offers an explanation: in the absence of the master the slave in charge takes advantage of his situation and misbehaves. His master will return unexpectedly and catch him with drunkards, having beaten his fellow slaves, and the master will punish him (Matt 24:45-51).

The image of sleep as opposed to watchfulness can be taken in a variety of directions. It works very differently from a sense of despair or powerlessness. Sleepiness may suggest a lack of purpose, or it may signal a false sense of well-being. Precisely how we are to hear the injunction to stay awake is best answered by reading on in the narrative, where only a little later, Jesus takes the same inner circle to watch with him while he prays immediately prior to his arrest. After his agonized prayer, Jesus returns to find his disciples asleep:

> And he said to Peter, "Simon, are you asleep? Could you not keep awake one hour? Keep awake and pray that you may not come into the time of trial; the spirit indeed is willing, but the flesh is weak."
>
> (14:37-38)

The scene is repeated three times; each time the disciples prove unable to stay awake. They have no sense of the impending danger. They can provide no support for their Master. They sleep as the forces of darkness gather. They are caught unprepared when the soldiers come to arrest Jesus. Despite their preparation for the time of trial, they collapse utterly. "All of them deserted him and fled" (14:50).

"What I say to you, I say to all," Jesus says. "Stay awake." Among the trials the future will bring, the temptation to fall asleep is apparently one of the greatest.

Lessons Learned

Jesus' teaching does little for the disciples. The instructions, given to the inner circle of the two pairs of brothers, do little to motivate action or shape the plot. While Jesus is accused at his trial of predicting the fall of the Temple (14:57-58), the wording has no obvious relationship to the prediction in 13:1-2. And Jesus' forecasts have no obvious impact on the disciples. When the tests come, the disciples are utterly unprepared and run away.

The discourse has a very different function for readers of the Gospel. It contributes a great deal to an appreciation of the story. That the chapter appears here, prior to the passion, means that the events of Jesus' trial and death are played out in the context of what is yet to come. In crucial ways his trial and death confirm his warnings: councils and synagogues and governors have no room for such a King as Jesus. The future of the movement is played out in what remains of his life as he is interrogated, beaten, and crucified. The need for watchfulness is likewise played out in the experience of his most intimate associates. The story confirms that the picture Jesus sketches of the world is truthful. The pattern may even extend to details. The darkness during the Crucifixion (15:33) at least echoes the promise that "the sun will be darkened" (13:24). Jesus' words to the chief priest, "And you will see the Son of man sitting at the right hand of Power, and coming with the clouds of heaven" (14:62 RSV), echo the promise about the return of the son of man in public view (13:26-27).

Jesus' discourse likewise plays an important role in our experience of the ending of the Gospel. Like the seed parables, his prophecies of what is to come interject momentum into the story. What is planted will surely produce a harvest. The onset of labor pains means that the future is even now making its presence felt in a real if uncomfortable way. Jesus' ministry is not only about a past and a present; it is about a future at the end of which stand the Son of Man and his angels, a future toward which the present strains. The future will include preaching the gospel as well as suffering, working within the household as well as giving testimony before governors and kings. Jesus' ministry has a future. An important question will be how that sense of future relates to an experience of the ending of the Gospel.

CHAPTER 7

THE DEATH OF THE KING

(14:43–15:47)

One-third of Mark's Gospel is devoted to an account of Jesus' last few days. One-sixth focuses on his last twenty-four hours. By itself the data is enough to indicate the centrality of these events for appreciating what it means that the story is "the good news of Jesus Christ."

A number of things will strike readers. One is that upon Jesus' arrival in Jerusalem, the pace of the story slows dramatically. While in the early going Jesus moves "immediately" from place to place, here his movements are plotted with care: "It was two days before the Passover and the festival of Unleavened Bread" (14:1); "On the first day of Unleavened Bread" (14:12); "at the third hour...at the sixth hour...at the ninth hour." Places are suddenly important: Bethany, the Mount of Olives, an upper room, the courtyard of the chief priest, the Pavement, Golgotha. Names appear, some for the first time, never to appear again: Simon of Cyrene, Alexander, Rufus, Joseph of Arimathea.

On the other hand, given the abundance of detail, nowhere in the story is the narrator's failure to provide information more striking. The mysterious instructions to the disciples about locating a colt for Jesus' entry into Jerusalem (11:2-6) and finding the upper room for Passover (14:12-15) suggest that plans have been made—if not by Jesus or the disciples, then by some divine agent. We learn nothing about the preparation, however. The "cleansing" of the Temple (11:15-17), a provocative act particularly during so inflammatory a time as Passover, is tersely narrated in a few verses, leaving historians to speculate about what Jesus had in mind and why he was not arrested immediately. Mysterious figures move in and out of the story, like the unnamed young man who runs away naked at Jesus' arrest (14:51-52). We learn that the disciples flee when Jesus is arrested (14:50)—with the exception of Peter, who follows only to deny Jesus three times. What happens to them, however, remains a mystery. The story closes before we learn (16:8). With so much at stake in their rehabilitation after the Resurrection, the silence is bewildering.

The case of Judas Iscariot is perhaps the most interesting. He is a notable figure with an important role in the plot. He betrays Jesus, giving the authorities an opportunity to arrest him in the absence of the crowds (14:10-11). No motivation of any sort is provided for him, however. The only thing we know about Judas is that he is identified as the one who betrayed Jesus in the initial list of the Twelve whom Jesus chose (3:19). And we learn nothing about what happens to him. It is not surprising that later traditions fill out the character: he was a thief (John 12:5-6); he was paid money to betray Jesus (Luke 22:3-5), in the amount of thirty pieces of silver (Matt 26:14-15); he died a terrible death, hanging himself (Matt 27:3-5), his bowels bursting (Acts 1:18); he was buried in a field he had purchased with the money (Acts 1:18-20) or that the Temple authorities purchased with the money (Matt 27:9-10). Such creativity has not ceased. Most modern Jesus literature—like *Jesus Christ Superstar*—achieves a real plot only by inventing a character for Judas: he was disillusioned; he was afraid Jesus had lost control. Particularly here, the lack of interest in character development is apparent. We are only told what happens, not why—and that "it is necessary."

On the one hand, the absence of information may serve as a useful reminder about the difficulty of reading at a distance. It is likely that the story of the "certain young man" who ran away naked (14:51-52) made sense to an early audience, who would probably also have known "Alexander and Rufus" whose father, Simon, carried Jesus' cross. Most readers of Mark's Gospel must make do without such information, however. Perhaps we can know nothing more than that it must have made sense to someone.

On the other hand, the author's failure to provide so much surface detail that seems necessary to make sense of the story may be understood as an indication of a different type of literature. Appreciating the narrative may require developing an appreciation for a different narrative strategy, not unlike studying the variety of ways visual artists have chosen to "re-present" reality on canvas.

WHAT EVER HAPPENED TO PETER?

While Peter was below in the courtyard, one of the servant-girls of the high priest came by. When she saw Peter warming himself, she stared at him and said, "You also were with Jesus, the man from Nazareth." But he denied it, saying, "I do not know or understand what you are talking about." And he went out into the fore-court. Then the cock crowed. And the servant-girl, on seeing him, began again to say to the bystanders, "This man is one of them." But again he denied it. Then after a little while the bystanders again said to Peter, "Certainly you are one of them; for you are a Galilean." But he began to curse, and he swore an oath, "I do not know this man you are talking about." At that moment the cock crowed for the second time. Then Peter remembered that Jesus had said to him, "Before the cock crows twice, you will deny me three times." And he broke down and wept. (Mark 14:66-72)

Auerbach's masterly *Mimesis* remains a classic in literary studies despite the many works that have followed. A student of literature, Auerbach was interested in the aesthetic vision of the Bible—in the case of the NT, of the Gospel according to Mark. His question was how storytellers sought to re-present reality. What counts as "realistic"? According to aesthetic traditions contemporary with Mark, "realism" consists in painting a complete surface on the canvas. Everything necessary to appreciate the story is there on the surface. In the opening chapter of the book, he compares the story of Abraham and Isaac in Genesis with Homer's *Odyssey,* noting how the latter "foregrounds" and the former does not. In the second chapter, he compares Mark's Gospel with the writings of Petronius and Tacitus.

In commenting on the story of Peter's denial, Auerbach asks how the author can have neglected so much. In particular, why are we not told what happens to Peter? The story leaves Peter in a difficult spot, hanging around the high priest's house where Jesus is condemned to death for blasphemy. He is recognized as one of Jesus' followers. Will he be arrested as well? And if he should escape, how will he live down his failure? Or in remorse does he do away with himself?

Interpreting the narrative includes awareness of its character. The story is not told, for example, from the perspective of any of the participants. The omniscient narrator locates the reader "above" the story where things appear different from the way they may appear to characters in the story. It is important, for example, that Peter's "interrogation" at the hands of servants occurs simultaneously with Jesus' trial before the chief priests, the elders, and the scribes. This sense of simultaneity is accomplished by moving back and forth from the courtyard, where Peter is warming himself, to the inside of the house where Jesus is being tried, back again to the courtyard. To be precise, Peter is questioned by the "female servant of the chief priest" while the high priest himself is asking Jesus the question that will lead to his condemnation: "Are you the Christ, the Son of the Blessed?" (RSV). Peter is asked simply, "Are you not with the Galilean, Jesus?" The two accounts play off against one another. Peter and Jesus provide foils for one another, each performance emphasizing the other. Jesus tells the truth, though it means his death; Peter lies, and in so doing saves his life. Their performance is reminiscent of something Jesus has already said:

> Those who want to save their life will lose it, and those who lose
> their life for my sake, and for the sake of the gospel, will save it.
>
> (8:35)

We shall see what that means for Peter.

There is more. After denying Jesus for the third time, Peter hears the rooster crow "for a second time." He recalls how Jesus had said to him, "Before the cock crows twice, you will deny me thrice" (there is a rhyme in the Greek). At that point he breaks down. The recollection means one thing for Peter: it is a sign of his failure to keep his word to Jesus ("Even though I must die with you, I will not deny you" [14:31]). It means something else for the reader, who can recall Jesus' explicit prediction in 14:28. Peter's collapse fulfills Jesus' prophecy. Jesus makes other prophetic statements in the same context. In 14:28-29, he predicts that his disciples will fall away, that Peter will deny him, and that he will precede them to Galilee when he is raised from the dead. The prophecy makes no impact on the disciples—but readers can appreciate what Jesus says, particularly when the prophecies about the disciples and Peter are fulfilled to the most minute detail (the second cock crow).

The trial narrative itself contains a prophetic statement from Jesus. In response to the question of the high priest, "Are you the Christ, the Son of the Blessed?" (RSV). Jesus said, "I am; and 'you will see the Son of Man seated at the right hand of the Power,' and 'coming with the clouds of heaven' " (14:62). The "servants" of the court call attention to that prophecy. After Jesus has been condemned, they taunt him: "Prophesy!" (14:65). The contrast between the one before them and one "seated at the right hand of the Power" is too great; it is the stuff of ridicule. Unknown to them, however, one of Jesus' prophecies is being fulfilled at that very moment, just outside in the courtyard. Readers understand what is happening in a way that is very different from the characters. The words mean different things in different settings. "Irony" is the appropriate term. Events are unfolding just as Jesus has predicted—and just as the prophets have announced. Characters in the story understand their roles only within their limited spheres and have no idea that they are playing roles assigned them by God.

Such observations are crucial to an appreciation of the story. They suggest, according to Auerbach, that the story offers another sense of what is "realistic." Events have depth. According to this new vision, we do not understand events without recognizing how different they may appear from another vantage point—in this case, from God's point of view. Characters in the story play their roles with no sense of what is "really" happening. Jesus goes "as it has been written of him." His "rejection" (Ps 118:22) at the hands of the authorities is "necessary." God's will is being carried out by people who have no comprehension of how their actions are serving that purpose.

"AS IT HAS BEEN WRITTEN"

One of the ways the narrator accomplishes this rhetorically is by employing the words of the scriptures in telling the story. While there are no quotations of the scriptures, set off by a formula like, "This was done in order to fulfill what was written in the Psalms" (except for 15:28, a verse that appears only as a footnote in modern Bible translations), there are allusions clear to anyone who knows the Greek Old Testament.

1. The religious authorities "reject" Jesus, according to his characterization in the first prediction of his death and resurrection in 8:31-33. The term appears in the citation of Psalm 118:22 in 12:11: "The stone that the builders *rejected* has become the cornerstone. This was the Lord's doing, and it is amazing in our eyes."
2. Jesus' response to the question of the chief priest, "You will see the Son of man sitting at the right hand of the Power and coming with the clouds of heaven," includes allusion to at least two passages (Ps 110:1 and Dan 7:13), possibly to three (Zech 12:10).
3. The comment that soldiers "cast lots" for Jesus' clothing uses the language of Psalm 22:18; that the crowds "shake their heads" alludes to 22:7; and Jesus' cry, "My God, my God...," is the opening line of the psalm.
4. The offer of vinegar alludes to Psalm 69:21.

There may be echoes of other scriptural passages. These are the clearest, since they all employ the exact words from the Greek Old Testament. The passages are not quoted, but the use of the words of scriptures is a kind of argument—even if not consciously intended. The events proceed according to a script. They are "necessary" in that they have been predicted. Readers can appreciate the story without knowing that there are echoes of Israel's scriptures, but the story takes on depth and richness when the allusions strike responsive chords. By using the actual words of the scriptures, the author allows readers to experience the scriptural character of the story (hence its "necessity").

"THE KING OF THE JEWS"

A consistent feature of the passion is that Jesus is tried, mocked, and finally executed as King. At the climax of his trial before the Jewish court, he is asked the critical question: "Are you the Christ, the Son of the Blessed?" (14:61 RSV). The language— "Son of the Blessed One" instead of "Son of God"—features proper Jewish sensitivity about using the name of God; "Blessed One" as a paraphrase is familiar particularly from rabbinic terminology. The use of the two titles, "Christ" and "Son of God," harks back to the opening verse of the Gospel. Here, for the first and only time in the story, the terms appear together—on the lips of Jesus' adversaries. Jesus' response—featuring images of one enthroned at God's right hand—belongs within the same royal ideology. That "the Christ" is a royal designation is confirmed in chapter 15, when another group of Jewish mockers taunt Jesus as "the Christ, the King of Israel" (15:32 RSV).

The trial before Pilate picks up the royal imagery, now from the perspective of Romans (non-Jews). In Israel's tradition, the King is "anointed" by God ("the Anointed One" translates "the Messiah" in Hebrew and "the Christ" in Greek). Romans are interested only in political implications. For them, the claim that Jesus is King is understood as "the King of the Jews." The title appears five times—three times on Pilate's lips, once in the mockery of the soldiers, and once in the inscription of the charge Pilate writes.

We learn several things from the narrative. One is that calling Jesus "Christ" or "King" sounds absurd to everyone. Religious and political leaders alike offer an appraisal of how the confession sounds. To the religious authorities, the claim to be "the Christ, the Son of the Blessed" (RSV), enthroned at God's right hand, is pretentious to the point of blasphemy. To the Romans the claim is seditious (there can be only one king in Caesar's realm) and absurd. The mockery reveals the view of the authorities.

The constant play on the royal imagery serves quite another purpose for readers who know that Jesus is "Christ, the Son of God": it provides testimony to the truth. If Jesus is really king, he should be invested—and so he is. Soldiers dress him in a royal robe and put a crown on his head, kneeling in homage: "Hail, King of the Jews!" (15:18). Pilate formulates the inscription: "The King of the Jews" (15:26). His enemies invest him as king and announce his identity—though in mockery, without understanding that they speak the truth. Contrary to their intentions, beyond their comprehension, they play a crucial role in the unconventional climax of the ministry of Jesus Christ, the Son of God.

In such a story, we may ask how we are to hear and play the role of the centurion who, at the most unlikely moment in the story, speaks the truth about Jesus: "Truly this man was God's Son!" (15:39). The traditional interpretation of the statement—that it is a confession by someone genuinely moved by Jesus' death—is not impossible. It would fit the pattern of surprising confessions familiar from earlier in the story, giving some anticipation of the ministry of the gospel to the "Gentiles," of which Jesus has spoken (13:10—"And the good news must first be proclaimed to all nations [= Gentiles]"). There is something about the traditional interpretation that is too convenient, however, for readers in need of some relief from the unrelenting gloom. Mark's sketch of the passion offers little "satisfaction." Jesus dies a failure in the eyes of his contemporaries, abandoned by the crowds, his followers, and finally even by God. His last cry, "My God, my God, why have you forsaken me?" (15:34) is misunderstood by the crowd as a call to Elijah (the words "my God" and "Elijah" sound similar in Mark's Greek); with that last misunderstanding, he dies. And if the "confession" of the centurion might seem to provide some relief, the narrative's end, with frightened women who say nothing to anyone, makes of this "opening" a temporary relief at best.

More interesting, I find, is a reading of the centurion's statement in light of the other "confessions" among Jesus' adversaries. Like the chief priest, the guards who taunt Jesus to prophesy, the mockers at the foot of the cross, Pilate, and the rest of the Roman soldiers, the centurion may say more than he knows. If the confession is sarcastic, it would fit the general tone of irony. Nothing in Jesus' ignominious death would convince anyone that he was the King. In fact, it would seem to be a final disqualification. There is ample motivation in the story for a last sarcastic comment by a soldier. And there is equally good reason for understanding how the last comment functions ironically as confirmation for readers who watch the story from another place, appreciating what players in the drama cannot. The confession of the centurion is true, whether or not he understands what he says. And in fact it is even more "true"—even more realistic—if he does not understand what he is saying. The narrative sketches a world in which things are not the way they appear, particularly to those in power. That sketch will probably strike most contemporary readers as true to the way things are.

Such a concern with the actual experience of reading, I should point out, shifts interest from within the story to this side of the printed page. Contemporary readers must finally give voice to the ancient narrative. The reaction of people to the ironic reading of the centurion is revealing. Most students, who like sarcasm, are quite open to the reading. Older, more established Bible readers are generally more skeptical. Exegetical arguments in favor of the "traditional" reading are not terribly convincing. The negative response usually has more to do with custom and a desire to keep interpretation under control. That a reader can change the experience of the story with an alteration in the voice is unsettling. A student, when pressed about his discomfort with the ironic reading, had to acknowledge that the "truth" of the centurion's confession did not depend upon whether or not the soldier knew what he was saying. What he didn't like was the loss of control. "I don't like it that you have the power to change the story by your tone of voice," he said. "I don't want to grant you that authority, and I surely don't want it for myself." Perhaps there are no alternatives, other than disinterested readings that are far more destructive and deadening than mistaken ones.

THE TEMPLE

At the moment of Jesus' ignominious death, two things occur: the centurion makes his "confession," and the Temple curtain is torn in two, "from top to bottom." Notable is the lack of explicit connection between the two events. Attempts to explain the centurion's statement as a reaction to the torn curtain are highly artificial. The "curtain" to which reference is made is probably the curtain in front of the Holy of Holies. Such an event would only be visible to those in the sanctuary. And even if we were to imagine another curtain, the narrative makes no explicit connection between the tearing and the centurion's declaration. Like the voice at Jesus' baptism, the narrator's words are for readers, not for participants in the story. We have no idea who saw the curtain or what they made of it. We know only that the curtain—like the heavens at Jesus' baptism—was torn. This time, however, the verb suggests a completed event. The curtain has been torn; it is finished.

The event is narrated without any interpretation. Readers are expected to make whatever sense of the event they can. Information about the actual layout of the Temple is helpful. Most commentators will point out that there was a curtain in front of the Holy of Holies, the most sacred precinct of the sanctuary behind which was the ark of the covenant with the tablets of the commandments inside. God was present in a special way in this precinct. No one could enter except the high priest, and he dared to enter only once a year, on the Day of Atonement. God's presence, as Jews knew, was dangerously holy. A glimpse of God meant death. Even the angels shielded their eyes.

At least as relevant is the information provided by the Gospel itself. The link with the tearing of the heavens we have explored earlier. Important here is that the Temple is mentioned on a number of occasions in the concluding chapters, and we may expect that the various comments are related.

In the first of these scenes, Jesus makes for the Temple upon his triumphant procession into Jerusalem (11:11). He does not enter its precincts until the next day, however, when he overturns the tables of merchants and money changers (11:15-16). Commentators often speak of Jesus' desire to rid the Temple of dishonest merchants, but the Gospel says nothing of this. What the event means seems to be captured in Jesus' "teaching": " 'My house shall be called a house of prayer for all the nations,' but you have made it a den of robbers [i.e., turned it into a "bandit's lair"]" (11:17).

Jesus' comment features two biblical passages: the first, from Isaiah 56, envisions a time when God's holy mountain will be a place to which everyone comes for refreshment. The oracle promises that there will be a place for everyone, even those Gentiles who observe the sabbath. God's house will be a house of prayer for all the nations (Gentiles).

The second passage is from Jeremiah 7, the prophet's famous Temple sermon in which he announces God's judgment on "this house, which is called by my name." Citing the precedent of the temple in Shiloh that was destroyed, Jeremiah promises that God will destroy the house in Jerusalem (i.e., the Temple) that has been turned into a bandit's hideout. The term usually translated as "robber" is more general; it surely does not mean dishonest merchant or thief.

> Will you steal, murder, commit adultery, swear falsely, make offerings to Baal, and go after other gods that you have not known, and then come and stand before me in this house, which is called by my name, and say, "We are safe!"—only to go on doing all these abominations? Has this house, which is called by my name, become a *den of robbers* in your sight?... Therefore I will do to the house that is called by my name, in which you trust, and to the place that I gave to you and to your ancestors, just what I did to Shiloh. And I will cast you out of my sight, just as I cast out all your kinsfolk, all the offspring of Ephraim. (Jer 7:9-15, emphasis added)

Jesus' "cleansing" of the Temple is really an announcement of its impending doom. Like the fig tree he curses because it does not yield fruit (a story that brackets the cleansing of the Temple in 11:12-14 and 11:20-25), the Temple will be destroyed.

The theme is explored in the following sections. Jesus tells a parable about tenants of a vineyard who will not pay their rent but kill the heir when he comes, hoping that they will thereby secure the vineyard for themselves (12:1-9). The leaders of the Temple perceive that Jesus told this parable "against them" (12:12).

In his glimpse of what is to come, Jesus states explicitly that the Temple will be destroyed. Not one stone will be left on another (13:1-2). The announcement of its impending doom leads to a longer forecast of what is in store for Jesus' followers.

At Jesus' trial, one of the charges brought against him—the only one to be mentioned in detail—is that Jesus had promised to destroy the Temple. The wording is precise: "We heard him say, 'I will destroy this temple that is made with hands, and in three days I will build another, not made with hands'" (14:58). The people who say such things are "testifying falsely." The reason their testimony does not secure Jesus' death is that they cannot agree. Yet their joint testimony is reported quite precisely. The tension is not explained.

While the charge does not secure Jesus' conviction, and while it is true that Jesus has never spoken precisely these words in the story, the charge is picked up again in the account of the mockery at the foot of the cross. "Aha! You who would destroy the temple and build it in three days, save yourself, and come down from the cross" (15:29-30). The wording is different from that at the trial; the taunters allege that Jesus promised the destruction and the rebuilding of the Temple—not the building of another temple, "not made with hands." The taunt reminds us, however, that the future of the Temple is one of the issues between Jesus and Israel's leaders.

At the moment of his death, the curtain tears—from top to bottom. There can be no doubt that the tearing is God's work. And in this context, there is enough momentum to connect the tearing of the curtain with the other references to the Temple. There are signs already at the moment of Jesus' death that the Temple is doomed. When the Jerusalem Temple was burned by the Romans some decades later, some of Jesus' partisans recalled that it was the Temple authorities who "rejected" Jesus. While he became "the head of the corner," the Temple was destroyed.

There is a question how much one ought to read into (or out of) the charge at Jesus' trial. The precise formulation of the charge, particularly the distinction between "this temple made with hands/another not made with hands" suggests the charge is not simply false testimony. There is enough evidence that Jesus' followers used the imagery of the Temple to speak of their community to see in the false testimony a prediction that Jesus will build a replacement for the Temple (1 Cor 3:10-17; 1 Pet 2:4-6; Eph 2:20-22). The "three days" is likely a reference to the Resurrection. That the Messiah might be expected to build a new temple at the end of days, from messianic passages like 2 Samuel 7:10-14 (esp. v. 12) and Zechariah 6:12, may indicate that the whole of the trial operates within messianic categories. More is needed to sustain such an argument.[1] Here it is sufficient to note the connection among the various statements made about the Temple. Jesus' death and the Temple are intimately related. While it is the Temple authorities who reject Jesus and hand him over, God will vindicate the rejected stone—and of the Temple not one stone will be left on another.

THE WAY IT IS

A traditional way of assessing the passion account is to ask what it means in doctrinal categories. What understanding of atonement is present here? What is the Christology of the passion? A different way of assessing the story is to ask aesthetic questions. In what sense, we might ask, is this story "realistic"? Artists in the various media differ both in their appraisal and in decisions they make about how to "represent" the real. At one point painters discovered that with certain "tricks," they could give the impression of depth in their paintings even though they were working on flat surfaces. Impressionists and expressionists offer varying notions of how to experience a simple scene in nature. Cubists rely on certain basic geometric shapes to which a scene is reduced. Artists might well have the ability to copy a photograph, but few would regard such reproduction as art. An artist can communicate something about a simple scene that brings out emotions that are "true" but not captured in a photograph. Of course even photographs can be "adjusted" as the technician wishes, something that digital photography has made even easier.

The account of Jesus' trial and death does more than reproduce facts. The story cannot be reduced to a series of propositions or doctrinal statements. It offers a sketch of reality. It portrays a world, and the world it portrays—the world it allows us to experience—is one in which there is far less stability than we may have imagined. Those entrusted with the task of guarding and applying the deepest moral principles—the leaders of the religious and political institutions—turn out to be blind. They have eyes but they cannot see. They judge by what is available to them, and in terms of all they know, Jesus is a dangerous pretender who is a threat to the tradition and to law and order. He is popular with the wrong sorts of people. The mere claim that he is the promised King is enough to put him out of the way. In view of their religious heritage and the law, the leaders condemn Jesus to death.

As privileged readers, we know what they could not have known. We have heard heavenly testimony about Jesus' identity, as well as "confessions" from supernatural powers (unclean spirits). We have been given glimpses of the divine script on the basis of which the story proceeds. Everything means something other than what it appears to mean, not in the sense of allegory but in terms of appraisal. Categories are inverted. Jesus is indeed the Christ, the King of Israel, the Son of the Blessed One, the King of the Jews. Yet his most royal moments occur in a setting that is utterly inappropriate to his office. Like his initial appearance among sinners in his baptism by John, Jesus' death as an insurrectionist and a would-be king would seem to be the end of his movement. Everyone who has invested something in Jesus has been disappointed. Nothing remains of his movement but a few women who wait to see where he is buried. Readers view the events from a different place, however. We know Jesus' death will not mark the end. Promises have been made. Jesus will not remain shut up in a grave. The Temple will be destroyed and a new temple constructed. That cannot conceal the fact, however, that the world is a place where appearance and truth can be confused—where there may still be a chasm between the "things of God" and "human things" (8:33).

Irony is tricky. Some may find irony comforting, a sign that we at least can appreciate the way things are. The same irony may be turned against readers, however. Discovery that the whole experience of the story can be changed by altering the tone of voice in which the centurion is played shakes the foundations and is itself part of the experience of "reality." As readers, we may be blind and deaf to colors and tones others must reveal to us.

One of the ways to avoid such surprises is to develop methods of interpretation that promise control. The desire to achieve stability through interpretation is perhaps understandable. It is possible, however, that such attempts to guarantee status as insiders will only yield to subsequent discoveries that unmask pretensions. It may be comforting to imagine there is a divine perspective from which the story can be viewed; it is pretentious to imagine that we can achieve it through interpretation. In this sense, reading Mark has some affinities to reading the literature of Kafka. Disappointment is an important part of the experience of engagement. Interpreting is discovering again and again that there are no ways to prevent the surprises and the unsettling recognition that we are not in control as interpreters. In theological terms, we might say this is a narrative experience of Paul's insistence that the "wisdom of the cross" is folly to the worldly.

EPILOGUE: SOME HISTORICAL REFLECTIONS

Is it true? Did Jesus' career end the way the Gospels portray it? Was he really condemned by the Jewish court, tried before the Roman procurator, found guilty, and executed? What actually happened? Historical questions would seem most important at this point of the story, where particular names and places are most prominent, and since the passion of Jesus is not only the central feature of Mark's Gospel but has formed the center of the Christian story over the centuries.

The story of Jesus' trial and death has been subjected to unprecedented scrutiny by historians of all sorts. A measure of the body of opinion is Raymond Brown's massive and masterful *The Death of the Messiah,* a two-volume work that gathers the most important scholarship on the central narrative of the Christian church and offers an interpretation and an assessment.[2] Brown takes on all the major questions, including the date of Jesus' trial: Was he executed on Passover (Matthew, Mark, and Luke) or on the day before, the Day of Preparation (John)? Did the Jewish court have the authority to try Jesus for a capital crime, or is the trial before the Sanhedrin mostly fictional? Does Jesus' death on a cross indicate that he made an attempt to seize power by force, or does the story play on the irony that the politically innocent Jesus is executed while a convicted insurrectionist (Barabbas) goes free? The care with which evidence is presented and discussed is a model for anyone interested in close reading and historical investigation.

I wish to deal with one feature of the story: the charge against Jesus that he is "the King of the Jews." The charge is interesting for several reasons. For one thing, it absolutely dominates the account of Jesus' trial and death, as we have seen. Jesus is tried, mocked, and executed as King (whether expressed in Jewish terms as "the Christ, the King of Israel," or in Roman terms as "the King of the Jews"). While others are crucified with Jesus, only he is executed as a would-be king. The royal imagery is striking, second, because of its almost complete absence from Jesus' public ministry. Jesus is identified as "Christ" (King) by no one besides Peter and the disciples (8:29). People observing his ministry draw analogies with prophetic figures like Moses or Elijah—not surprisingly, since Jesus' ministry of teaching with authority and displaying "signs and wonders" is precisely what typified prophets like Elijah and would characterize the ministry of the "prophet like Moses" whose return was expected. Despite numerous attempts to make sense of Jesus' ministry in "messianic" terms, thus far no convincing arguments have been advanced to link Jesus' teaching and healing with what was expected of the Messiah-King when he would come at the end of days.

At this point some knowledge of Israel's visions and dreams of the future is helpful. A large volume of essays edited by James Charlesworth, entitled *The Messiah,* makes the point convincingly.[3] In the century prior to the Christian era numerous visions and dreams of the future developed, all making use of various scriptural passages. Some expected a future in which there would be a high priest at the head of the community, others a prophet like Moses, still others a priest and a king. The extant literature indicates there was no consensus, no "normative" view of the future. Those whose vision was shaped by biblical verses in the royal tradition, like Psalm 2, Isaiah 11, 2 Samuel 7:10-14, and Genesis 49:10, were only one group among many. And those who expected that God would send a Messiah-King to liberate Israel surely did not expect that the Lord's Messiah would die.

Mark's story makes the point, and it is confirmed by a study of Jewish literature: nothing about Jesus' early ministry indicated that he was the promised Messiah, and the climax of his ministry—his death—would have ruled out the possibility for everyone. The authorities thought the claim absurd, something worthy of ridicule. And the Gospel story does not try to conceal the reality. In fact, it plays on it. Jesus is most consistently depicted as King when he looks least like a king.

One may ask the historical question: Is there a chance anyone would have made up such a story? Invention at this point is most unlikely. That Jesus is the promised King sent by God to deliver Israel would not have occurred to people. And even if God raised Jesus from the dead, nothing would necessarily suggest that he was the risen Messiah. His followers could as easily have spoken of him simply as "the living Jesus," or the vindicated prophet (using language from the story of Elijah, who was taken up into heaven). God's vindication of the crucified Jesus would be understood as the vindication of the crucified King only if Jesus had been executed as King. What would have suggested that the story of Jesus be told as the story of the crucified—and risen—King of the Jews unless that is actually what occurred? Why would Jesus' followers have used the designation "Messiah" (Christ) with such frequency, knowing how little it suited what actually occurred in Jesus' ministry, unless they were obliged by the facts to use it?

According to this reconstruction, once the confession of Jesus as Messiah is made, interpreters can explore its significance, once hidden but now revealed. The apostle Paul could argue that God's unexpected, even scandalous involvement in the career of the promised Christ is crucial to understanding the good news: Jesus' shameful death on the cross exposes the distance between the wisdom of God and human wisdom, to which the wisdom of God appears as foolishness (1 Cor 1:18–2:2). But why would any-one have invented the title as part of the story? Its use is so unprecedented, so contrary to what is told of Jesus' ministry, that it must be historical.

The most substantial historical "fact" in the account of Jesus' ministry is the charge Pilate formulated: Jesus is executed as "the King of the Jews," a would-be Messiah.

This leaves other questions to investigate. Did Jesus know he was the "Messiah" in such an unconventional sense? At what point in his career did he realize that? How much did he explain to his followers? It is a bit difficult to imagine that Jesus' follow-ers would have continued to confess him as "the Christ" if Jesus had been utterly opposed to the notion. The Gospel writers are nevertheless quite reserved in the matter of what Jesus knew and thought. The one matter on which they all agree is that when the question was put to him by the religious and political leaders, "Are you the Christ (King of the Jews)," he did not deny it. Precisely what he thought, however, is simply not available to us. The absence of such detailed information in the New Testament apparently means the writers did not regard it as crucial.

Detailed study of such questions must be left for another occasion. Most such questions cannot be answered. If part of interpretation is asking historical questions, however, this is a place where evidence is available and arguments can be made.

And at the point of the story's climax, there is good reason to imagine that things happened much as they are narrated—that Jesus died as "King of the Jews" at the hands of the Roman Prefect, Pontius Pilate, after having been handed over by the Jerusalem authorities.

CHAPTER 8

THE DEATH OF JESUS AND THE WILL OF GOD: A THEOLOGICAL APPRAISAL

That Jesus' death is a major feature of his ministry should be obvious. Not only does the account of his trial and death dominate the narrative, but from the very beginning of the story it is clear that Jesus' ministry is headed for a confrontation that will require a death. He is born to die.

We have also noted that in Mark, his death is not an accident. He tells his disciples that "the Son of Man *must* . . . be rejected by the elders, the chief priests, and the scribes" (8:31, emphasis added). Christian traditions have invested considerable effort in understanding the nature of that "necessity." "Necessity" is in part an argument about the interpretation of the Scriptures: Jesus goes "as it is written of him" (14:21). The host of allusions to the Old Testament serve as a kind of argument that, as Paul says,

157

quoting an ancient confession, "Christ died for our sins in accordance with the scriptures" (1 Cor 15:3). Since God stands behind the scriptures, "according to the scriptures" also means "according to the will of God."

Jesus' death must be understood in light of the will of God. The matter is stated explicitly in Jesus' prayer just before his arrest in the Garden of Gethsemane:

> And going a little farther, he threw himself on the ground and prayed that, if it were possible, the hour might pass from him. He said, "Abba, Father, for you all things are possible; remove this cup from me; yet, not what I want, but what you want." (14:35-36)

That God does not rescue Jesus after his agonized prayer suggests that his death is according to the will of God. Such observations raise important additional questions: What does it mean that the Crucifixion is "according to the will of God," and what are the implications for a reading of Mark's Gospel?

The use of scriptural (Old Testament) material to tell the story of Jesus' death is testimony to the conviction that it "has been written." The scriptural allusions do not attempt to give the reasons, however; they do not yield a theory about Jesus' death. They do not explain why God chose this way and not another. The task of offering such explanations has fallen to church tradition, which has fashioned various "theories of atonement." In many cases, however, these "theories" take little account of the particulars in the Gospel story—all the more reason for a close reading of the narrative.

These theories about Jesus' death, particularly the formulation of Anselm of Canterbury, have had an extraordinary impact on the shape of Christian imagination and in effect determine how the biblical story is experienced.[1] The theories are important because they have not remained scholarly formulations but have taken shape in cathedral windows, hymns, liturgies, and prayers. In the Middle Ages all these artistic media determined how people heard the Bible. Even if the influence of the church and ecclesiastical art is diminished in our culture, such theories still determine how the Bible is read. Here, perhaps more than anywhere, it is important to deal explicitly with what passes for theological "common sense" as it affects the reading and interpretation of

Mark's Gospel. How is God involved in the ministry of Jesus, particularly in his death? Why did Jesus have to die, and in what sense is it God's will?

When read with that question in mind, we may observe first that there is in Mark's Gospel remarkably little of the imagery Christian tradition has found most helpful in making sense of Jesus' death. Considering how important the language of sacrifice and atonement has been in the history of the Christian church, the virtual absence of the imagery from the lengthy story of Jesus' death is noteworthy. There is little "atonement" language in the whole Gospel. An exception is 10:45, where Jesus speaks about giving his life as a "ransom" for many. The metaphor is not developed. Does this mean that people are in bondage and their freedom must be purchased? If so, to whom are they in bondage and to whom is payment due? Various theories of atonement have made such questions central. In the Gospel narrative, they are not.

The other passage where such language is mentioned is in the account of Jesus' last meal with his followers. There he speaks of "my blood of the covenant, which is poured out for many" (14:24). Once again little context is provided for the provocative imagery. Some have proposed reading the account in light of Passover traditions (to the degree that they can be reconstructed for the first century), since Mark's Gospel notes that Jesus' last meal is a celebration of Passover. Such investigations have met with mixed reviews, particularly since the killing of the Passover lamb was not traditionally viewed as a sacrificial act.

Less hypothetical is relating the image to OT passages:

Moses took the blood and dashed it on the people, and said, "See the blood of the covenant that the LORD has made with you in accordance with all these words." (Exod 24:8)

As for you also, because of the blood of my covenant with you,
I will set your prisoners free from the waterless pit. (Zech 9:11)

The imagery may likewise allude to the famous verses from Jeremiah that speak of a "new covenant with the house of Israel and the house of Judah" (Jer 31:31-34). That allusion would seem clearer in Matthew, however, where Jesus speaks of "my blood of the [a variant reading adds "new"] covenant, which is poured out for many for the forgiveness of sins" (Matt 26:28).

Even if we grant that Jesus' words in Mark echo any or all of these scriptural texts, however, they do little to explain why Jesus must die and why his blood is necessary. While the Old Testament speaks regularly about sacrifice and blood, it does not offer a coherent theory of how and why sacrifice works.

"THE DEEP MAGIC"

The logic by which Jesus' death is understood as a "sacrifice," as noted above, has been provided by church theologians, among whom Anselm of Canterbury (1033–1109) stands out. His work *Cur Deus Homo?* (Why Did God Become Man?) has shaped the imagination of Christian readers ever since it was written.[2] His influence cannot be underestimated. His theory, as with most traditional arguments about the Atonement, locates the need for Jesus' death in the ultimate character of reality—that is, in God.

One of the most creative and accessible interpretations of these doctrines is found in the first of C. S. Lewis's *Narnia Chronicles* entitled *The Lion, the Witch, and the Wardrobe.*[3] The story is not simply an allegorical reading of the Gospel narrative, but it does seek to shed light on the meaning of the Christian story through a fictive invention. I have found Lewis's work useful as an entrée to the whole topic of atonement because it focuses the questions so nicely and because it has been so widely read. His work performs the same function as church art and music, taking biblical themes and offering interpretations in accessible media—in this case, in children's stories.

In the first volume of the *Narnia Chronicles,* the main characters are three children who find their way into the land of Narnia. The first major adventure includes being caught up in a battle between good and evil. The hero, clearly a Christ-figure, is Aslan, a lion. His antagonist is the White Witch. The story builds to a great confrontation between Aslan and his forces and the Witch and hers.

The major complication in the battle is a defection by a central figure in the story, one of Aslan's friends, the human child Edmund, who is tempted beyond his strength by the witch and betrays his friends. That defection, the story explains, gives the witch rights over the child.

"You have a traitor there, Aslan," said the Witch. Of course everyone present knew that she meant Edmund. But Edmund had got past thinking about himself after all he'd been through and after the talk he'd had that morning. He just went on looking at Aslan. It didn't seem to matter what the Witch said.

"Well," said Aslan. "His offense was not against you."

"Have you forgotten the Deep Magic?" asked the Witch.

"Let us say I have forgotten it," answered Aslan gravely. "Tell us of this Deep Magic."

"Tell you?" said the Witch, her voice growing suddenly shriller. "Tell you what is written on that very Table of Stone which stands beside us? Tell you what is written in letters deep as a spear is long on the trunk of the World Ash Tree? Tell you what is engraved on the scepter of the Emperor-Beyond-the-Sea? You at least know the magic which the Emperor put into Narnia at the very beginning. You know that every traitor belongs to me as my lawful prey and that for every treachery I have a right to a kill."

"Oh," said Mr. Beaver. "So *that's* how you came to imagine yourself a Queen—because you were the Emperor's hangman. I see."

"Peace, Beaver," said Aslan, with a very low growl.

"And so," continued the Witch, "that human creature is mine. His life is forfeit to me. His blood is my property."

"Come and take it then," said the Bull with the man's head in a great bellowing voice.

"Fool," said the Witch with a savage smile that was almost a snarl, "do you really think your master can rob me of my rights by mere force? He knows the Deep Magic better than that. He knows that unless I have blood as the Law says all Narnia will be overturned and perish in fire and water."

"It is very true," said Aslan; "I do not deny it."

"Oh, Aslan!" whispered Susan in the Lion's ear. . . . "Can't we do something about the Deep Magic? Isn't there something you can work against it?"

"Work against the Emperor's magic?" said Aslan turning to her with something like a frown on his face. And nobody ever made that suggestion to him again.[4]

According to the "deep magic," the only alternative to death for Edmund is for someone to take his place. The rules demand blood, and against such deep magic, which the Emperor himself has written, there can be no opposition. So Aslan volunteers to take the child's place. He must die because the deep magic requires it. In a gruesome scene, he is shaved and humiliated by the witch and her horde before being killed. His blood will atone for Edmund's crime, but how will it help in the long run? The witch herself makes the argument:

> And now, who has won? Fool, did you think that by all this you would save the human traitor? Now I will kill you instead of him as our pact was and so the Deep Magic will be appeased. But when you are dead what will prevent me from killing him as well? And who will take him out of my hand *then?* Understand that you have given me Narnia forever; you have lost your own life and you have not saved his. In that knowledge, despair and die.[5]

Lewis does not seek to sentimentalize the death of the Christ-figure. There is no nobility in death. The great lion dies alone, his friend Edmund asleep, unaware of what is taking place. And the reader must suffer at least the temporary despair of knowing that even his death is a stopgap measure, an ultimate failure. Yet death cannot be the end for the forces of good. Readers will hardly be surprised when Aslan is raised to life and is able to lead the forces of good against the forces of darkness. At this point the argument of the story strains to make sense. The rules required Aslan's death; they also explain his return to life. There is no violation of the rules, the Lion argues; in fact, his resurrection is required by the "deep magic":

> Though the Witch knew the Deep Magic, there is a magic deeper still which she did not know. Her knowledge goes back only to the dawn of Time. But if she could have looked a little further back, into the stillness and the darkness before Time dawned, she would have read there a different incantation. She would have known that when a willing victim who had committed no treachery was killed in a traitor's stead, the Table would crack and Death itself would start working backwards.[6]

The allegory attempts to explain why the king must die. Like most theories about Jesus' death, it does not spend much time with the particulars of the Gospel narratives but works with abstractions. The "deep magic" here represents the Law—to which everyone is subject, even the Emperor and his emissary. If God were to alter the law, according to this theory, the whole created order would return to chaos. There must be justice—and that, according to these theories, is what the Gospel story is about. Jesus "must" die because God is somehow obligated, whether to the law or the executioner. According to this reading, Christ is not the end of the law but its absolute confirmation—its victim. What endures forever is the deep magic, the law, to which even God is finally subject.

While such theories make a kind of sense, they do so by making God's actions fit into a pattern of justice that is the most theoretical aspect of the construct. God is made subject to a law humans have imagined. The result of this imagined pattern of justice is a God who demands blood in order to be merciful. The sketch does not square with biblical portraits, though it has shaped the way many read them. Closer attention to the particulars of the Gospel narrative can result in a rather different theory about why Jesus must die—one which is more sensitive to biblical stories and images.

BEYOND THE BOUNDARIES

To put the matter simply, Mark's Gospel does not ground the need for Jesus' death in God's obligations. God does not require blood in order to be merciful. Reflections on the "necessity" of his death begin not by looking at ultimate reality from God's point of view but "from below." The reasons for Jesus' death arise from his conflict with those in charge of human affairs, the religious and political authorities. It is their need to live within the bounds of the law that requires Jesus' execution. The Gospel's argument is that the human situation requires Jesus' death. People can only react to Jesus' graciousness with violence. And in this situation, not even the law can help. If there is to be deliverance, it will have to be—to use Paul's expression from Romans—"apart from Law" (Rom 3:21).

Far from depicting Jesus as a champion of the law, the story depicts him as transgressing boundaries. Jesus does not overthrow the law, but he presses at its boundaries, interpreting with an almost sovereign freedom. His apparent carelessness about sabbath regulations worries the religious who take the law seriously. His willingness to eat with sinners and tax collectors undermines moral resolve. His pronouncements about true family threaten the most basic structures of the society. His willingness to speak on his own authority, without guarantee of precedent, challenges the organization of authority within the religious and political communities. The mere fact that some believe Jesus to be "the King of the Jews" makes him a potential catalyst for rebellion.

Most serious of all is his willingness to speak and act on God's behalf. His declaration that "your sins are forgiven" early in the story elicits a charge of blasphemy from the scribes (2:6-7). The law is God's structure for life. The most important boundary is that between the divine and the human. Jesus transgresses all the boundaries, including the one that clearly distinguishes between God and the creature—and punishment for blasphemy, the ultimate transgression, is death.

Those who finally condemn Jesus to death are the religious and political authorities, those responsible for interpreting and enforcing the laws that hold the world together: the scribes, chief priests, and elders, who speak for the Jewish tradition, and Pilate, who speaks for Roman law. The story so constructs the world as to require a choice between Jesus and the tradition. That Jesus fulfills the will of God in a higher sense may be something apparent in retrospect, but it is of little help to those in the story who must interpret and choose. Jesus must die because he threatens the very possibility of organized religious and political life. He is either the one in whom truth is present, or he is the most dangerous sort—a charismatic personality with real power who will finally lead people astray into religious and political chaos.

According to the Gospel narrative, Jesus "must" die because people have no alternative. Like Peter, they are fixed on human ways and not on God's ways. Eyes and ears are shut; hearts are hardened. In such a situation, the law cannot deliver. It can achieve a measure of stability—but finally only by offering leaders a means of defending themselves against the possibility that Jesus is the one in whom God intrudes into the world of the everyday.

That Jesus dies, and that God makes of the rejected stone "the head of the corner," requires a fundamental reappraisal of everything, as it did for Paul when he discovered that those he persecuted were right after all (Phil 3:4-11). As the crucified and risen King, Jesus is both the revealer of God's graciousness and the surprise that exposes blindness and hardness of heart and bondage where no one knew they existed.

If there is an understanding of atonement in Mark's Gospel, it proceeds from the particulars of Jesus' career to infer what must be the case in the world for such a thing as Jesus' death to have occurred. Jesus must die not because God requires blood or is obligated to someone or something, but because God is gracious and is willing to suffer the consequences of becoming vulnerable. The narrative provides not so much a lesson about the value of suffering as an opportunity to experience the surprise in the career of Jesus the holy man, healer, preacher, and prophet—but most of all the crucified and risen King of the Jews. There is need for atonement because the world has no place for Jesus. When Jesus will not go away, the authorities must take measures to protect themselves and their traditions and their laws. Violence is the only possible end: they must kill to protect themselves.

The story argues that in this One, God accomplishes what the law cannot. God does not require Jesus' death but allows it. Everything depends on how God will respond. If the story offers promise, it is because God will not accept the verdict pronounced on Jesus. That God raises Jesus from the dead both puts the seal of approval on his ministry and demonstrates that there is no limit to God's will to show mercy. Violence and rejection are repaid not by more violence but by an act of God that makes all things new. And if the story gives a truthful depiction of the world—if liberation requires a confrontation that demands Jesus' death—it will also mean dramatic changes in the religious and political contexts when God vindicates the crucified Christ. "New skins for new wine."

CHAPTER 9

ENDINGS AND
BEGINNINGS

WHAT SHALL WE READ?

Interpreting Mark's Gospel requires decisions, none of which is any more important than the decision about what to read as the ending. Those who know only English and read only the King James Bible will have a less complicated encounter with Mark. According to the KJV, Mark ends with verse 20 in chapter 16, and with an "Amen." Modern translations must make choices, however, from alternatives not available to the king's translators at the end of the seventeenth century, most of which boast greater antiquity in terms of manuscript attestation. These alternatives—there are five—require knowledge of textual criticism and a decision.[1]

16:1-8
16:1-8 + the "longer ending" (vv. 9-20 in the KJV)
16:1-8 + the "shorter ending"
16:1-8 + the "longer" and the "shorter" endings
16:1-8 + the "longer" ending, with an additional comment about the unbelief of the disciples (from a single manuscript)

While some may view textual criticism as a way of getting back to the "original" Gospel of Mark, its first task is far more basic and ordinary: someone must decide what to print and thus what we shall read as the ending of the Gospel. Committees must decide which among the alternatives is the most reasonable text. On this issue there is little question among scholars. The most reasonable alternative is the one that ends the Gospel with 16:8: "And they said nothing to anyone, for they were afraid." That such a version exists at all is remarkable, given the pressure for copyists to make sense of what they copy. And that the versions of Mark with nothing after 16:8 appear in some of the most valuable manuscripts whose reliability has been demonstrated on other grounds makes the readings even more significant. Given the principles that the most difficult reading is generally to be preferred, the shortest is generally to be preferred, and one should choose the reading that can explain the others, 16:8 is the reasonable choice. It is the shortest, it is certainly the most difficult, and it is easy to see why a copyist would have been motivated to add something to Mark if it ended without a word from the frightened women.

Deciding what to do with the textual information is more difficult. Throughout most of its history, the church has read a version of Mark that ends with 16:20. While Jerome knew versions of Mark that concluded earlier, he chose for his Latin Vulgate the version that includes the longer ending. When the Vulgate became the Bible of the Roman Catholic Church—officially in 1548 but far earlier in practice—the form of Mark's Gospel was determined. But what does that history of use mean for making textual decisions? Historical precedent is important. But what weight will it be assigned in view of the textual evidence? Given the near certainty that Mark's Gospel was consciously altered by scribes who could not tolerate the open and disappointing ending, should we choose to read the edited version nevertheless because of its prominence in the history of the church? Such precedent would suggest that every textual decision should be made based on historical practice—and the whole point of textual criticism has been to "correct" the text of the Bible based on superior manuscript evidence.

Most troubling is that translation committees have not made public arguments for their choices and have not really offered

English readers a clear glimpse of the most reasonable form in which Mark comes to us. Further, publishers have participated in the conspiracy, printing evidence with such headings as "the longer ending" and "the shorter ending" that are misleading at best. To be consistent in practice, the alternative endings ought to appear in footnotes with the caption, "Other ancient authorities add." While careful readers may note the use of double brackets in the NRSV and can read the extended footnotes, most ordinary Bible readers who reach the end of Mark's Gospel will assume that one should choose between "the longer ending" and "the shorter ending"—and will do so based on their own taste.

We will proceed on the conviction that of the various forms of Mark's ending available to us, the most reasonable is the one that concludes the Gospel with verse 8. While it is possible that the "original" version had a different ending, we will work with what we have before inventing hypotheses of lost endings.

READING THE ENDING

The narrative has prepared for the events of Sunday morning even if the women have not. The story carefully details how Jesus' body was removed from the cross, wrapped in a linen cloth, and laid in a tomb. The narrator comments that at least two women—Mary Magdalene and Mary the mother of Joses—saw where the body was buried. The reason for the lack of proper preparation of the body is likewise offered by the narrator: evening was dawning, and with the setting of the sun the sabbath began. While preparing bodies for burial was one of the circumstances that could justify work on the sabbath in the later rabbinic codes, Joseph of Arimathea and the women are portrayed as scrupulous observers of the sabbath. Only after the sabbath is over—at sundown on Saturday—do the women purchase spices (16:1). Jewish tradition still provides the order and the structure of the action. Like the women, Joseph is introduced for the first time, to disappear once again after performing his necessary service. He is identified as "a respected member of the council, who was also himself waiting expectantly for the kingdom of God" (15:43). It is not clear why he assumes responsibility for burying Jesus' body.

The characters in the brief account of the empty tomb are three women, including Mary Magdalene and Salome. The other "Mary" is identified a bit differently in the references at 15:40 and 47. Unlike the male disciples, who have fled, they have remained to see where Jesus was buried and have gone on Sunday morning to do their duty in anointing the body. Several features of the story are strange. The women go with spices they have purchased, even though they know that a large stone seals the tomb and have no idea how they will remove it. When they find the stone has been rolled back, they enter the tomb to find Jesus gone and a "young man in a white robe" sitting on the right. Matthew and Luke both understand the figure as a heavenly messenger. In Matthew, the angel of the Lord descends from heaven and rolls back the stone. "His appearance was like lightning, and his clothing white as snow" (28:3). In Luke, "two men in dazzling clothes" appear to the women, and later we are told that the women saw a "vision of angels" (24:23). The terror of the women in Mark suggests that we are to understand the young man as a heavenly messenger, but the term is not "angel" and is interesting. "Young man" *(neaniskos)* is used only one other time in Mark to refer to the "young man" who ran away naked as Jesus was arrested (14:51-52). Some commentators have suggested a relationship between these two "young men," one naked and the other clothed. If so, making sense of the relationship is left almost entirely to the readers' imaginations.

In a story full of secrets, someone is finally instructed to tell: "tell the disciples, even Peter, that he is preceding you to Galilee. There you will see him, just as he told you." The brief glimpse of light is immediately obscured by clouds of mystery for one last time:

> So they went out and fled from the tomb, for terror and amazement had seized them; and they said nothing to anyone, for they were afraid. (16:8)

The ending is quite unsatisfying. Too many things are left unresolved. We cannot fail to note, however, that a number of important things occur. For one, Jesus' promise of resurrection is fulfilled. If the women are uncertain about what the empty tomb means, readers cannot be. On five separate occasions Jesus has promised that he would be raised "after three days" (8:31; 9:6;

170

9:33; 10:33; 14:28). His absence from the tomb suggests that readers should believe not only his promise of his death but of resurrection as well. The words of the "young man" echo explicitly Jesus' promise in 14:28, where he prophesies the scattering of the disciples, Peter's denial, and his preceding the group to Galilee. "Just as he told you," says the young man. Jesus' predictions echo through the narrative—not only the ones in which he promised he would meet his disciples, but others as well that await fulfillment: "Nothing is hidden except to be revealed"; "Do not speak to anyone of these things until after the son of man is raised from the dead"; "the gospel must first be preached to all the nations." The story has invested a great deal in Jesus' predictions, and the concluding emphasis on what he has said surely directs attention to those things yet to happen. The empty tomb thus indicates new birth from death. Jesus and his story have a future. The end is not yet.

What changes everything is the women's fear and their failure to tell. It is possible, of course, to add "at least not right away" to the narrative as a qualification of the disappointment. They must have told someone. That the story can be recounted at all presumes that someone spoke. The Gospel, however, resists resolution in a way that is genuinely troubling. The efforts of copyists and interpreters to bring the text to satisfying closure are a measure of its effects. It is not a satisfying ending. It is also not an "ending" in a sense that it wraps things up and finishes the story. Readers are left with unfulfilled promises and silent witnesses.

"THOSE WITH EARS TO HEAR"

What is at issue is the experience of actual readers. Endings are important because they do something to readers. They offer satisfaction by tying up loose ends, or they frustrate by not doing so.[2] They may surprise or shock. Interpretation must deal not only with what these verses mean but how they function as the conclusion to a narrative. If we ask about content, the problem is less obvious. The brief account provides testimony that Jesus has been raised, that death has not succeeded in silencing him, that God will not allow things to end here. But it does so in a way that is not finally satisfying. There is no proper "sense of an ending" here, no closure, no resolution. That is all the more apparent when the story is heard aloud, particularly when these verses conclude a performance of the entire Gospel that has lasted for almost two hours.

These observations are derived more from watching performers of the Gospel and audience reaction than from close reading of the text. A young man who had prepared for several years to perform Mark did so for the first time before a student body at the school where I taught. His performance was very effective. In his changing of position on the stage, shift in tone of voice, and occasional pauses, the Gospel story made good sense and came to life. One of the things he had decided, after studying the matter, was that he would end with 16:8. He had not anticipated what the experience would be like, however, and what he would do when he had finished his recitation. The performance was held in a large church sanctuary, out in front of the altar. He was standing before the audience when he spoke the last lines: "And they said nothing to anyone, for they were afraid." When he had finished, he stood awkwardly, obviously trying to decide how to end so that he could make an exit. Finally, after several seconds, he said, "Amen!" It seemed appropriate to the ecclesial setting. There was obvious relief within the audience, and people applauded enthusiastically. Later, we had a conversation in which it became clear to the performer that he had felt obliged to do what all of the later endings of the Gospel had done: to provide a sense of closure for the audience. Performance rituals for actors and audience, with the customary bows and applause, provide that sense of an ending that seems satisfying.

The next time he performed the Gospel, he tried something different. When he finished the last line, he paused for a few seconds, then simply exited. There was no "Amen" to bring the performance to a close; there was no applause to bring the evening to a proper end. The discomfort and uncertainty within the audience were obvious, and as people exited the sanctuary the buzz of conversation was dominated by the experience of the nonending.

Such experiences make suddenly clear that in most cases, interpretation becomes a way of trying to achieve satisfaction from an unsatisfying experience—like awakening from an uncomfortable dream and spending the next minutes trying to provide an ending before drifting back into sleep. One of the time-honored approaches to dealing with the Markan conclusion is to postulate a lost ending. Even sophisticated text critics who acknowledge that there is no justification for reading any of the alternative endings or printing them as "the" text of Mark insist that there must have been a lost ending, since a book cannot end in this fashion.

There is no evidence for a lost ending of Mark, though the view has been stated often enough to make it sound believable. Some argue that a Gospel cannot end as Mark does. Matthew and Luke are cited as comparisons. Yet if Matthew and Luke rewrote Mark, as most scholars assume, their revision of the ending indicates no common source but a shared uneasiness. Like the unknown scribes who sought to "fix" Mark's Gospel by providing other endings, Matthew and Luke offer their own corrections. Neither ends the story of Jesus, of course. Matthew concludes with Jesus' promise "to be with you to the close of the age"; Luke speaks of Jesus' departure and prepares for the continuation of the story in Acts. Nevertheless, both give readers a kind of satisfaction Mark does not. In Matthew, the women meet Jesus and actually touch him. The disciples are led to a mountain, and even their doubts are settled by Jesus' authoritative words and presence. In Luke, Jesus appears, gives lessons in the interpretation of the scriptures, and even offers to eat in the disciples' presence.

Such endings are subsequent to Mark, however, and seem to provide evidence that the versions of the story both authors shared concluded with the account of the empty tomb. Why could Mark not end at this point? The study of precedent in the Greco-Roman and Jewish worlds is inconclusive. Until other evidence is adduced, it seems reasonable to read 16:8 as the ending and to try out interpretations. That seems preferable to inventing a Gospel to interpret.[3]

PROMISES KEPT, PROMISES NOT KEPT

One of the habits of interpretation, obvious among commentators, is to approach difficulties in the text as problems to be solved. What does the disappointing ending require of us? What are we expected to do in the face of the women's frightened silence? The assumption is that some particular effort will bring the story to a more satisfying conclusion.

Interpretation is something we can do. "Solving the problem" of the ending becomes a task for interpreters. One interpretation is that the Gospel constructs us as ideal readers. Benefiting from the failure of the disciples and the silent women, we can succeed where they failed. We can speak where the women were silent. Our "Amen" can make of the story something satisfying rather than disappointing.

> The Gospel is open ended, for the outcome of the story depends on decisions which the church, including the reader, must still make.[4]

> The story *in* the Gospel seems to preclude the telling *of* the Gospel; Mark's Gospel is the story of a story that was never told. If we read the Gospel with a fixation on the story level, this ending may strike us as an immense problem. No problem exists, however, if we grant that this narrative is more concerned about discourse than story. The women may never tell the story of which they are a part, but the reader has read their story and can respond to it in a multitude of ways, among them the option of telling the story of the story that was never told. The burden of response-ability lies wholly on those of us standing outside the story.[5]

Such proposals have a certain attraction, but upon closer inspection they seem unconvincing. On what basis are present readers to trust that they can succeed as disciples where Jesus' chosen group failed? If the disciples' problem is that their hearts have been hardened, their eyes unseeing and their ears unhearing, what is to guarantee that we see and hear? While the experience of irony throughout the Gospel has forced us to adopt the role of insiders, knowing what characters in the story cannot, what is to guarantee that the future unfolding before us will not prove as opaque as it proved to be for the religious and political authorities—and even for the disciples?

Such an approach says a great deal about interpreters and interpretation, as Frank Kermode has so eloquently argued in his *Genesis of Secrecy.* Interpretation, he argues, is the way we get satisfaction from what may be impenetrable texts and an "unfollowable world."[6] It is an effort to reduce reality to an understandable algebra, to capture meaning in a formula. Kermode's relentless deconstruction of interpretations and his exposure of the desperation with which people pursue strategies that promise to get hold of texts arise from his conviction that in the end our creative involvement with texts is a way of getting temporary satisfaction in the face of the overwhelming sense of the impenetrability of life's mysteries. Interpretations can be sustained, finally, only by cunning and violence.

Remarkably, our instincts direct us away from the real promise in the story. The account of the empty tomb says nothing that awakens confidence in human characters. It would seem to be a final blow to such confidence. Even the women, who display a courage not present among the disciples, fail at the end. No one—not members of Jesus' own family, not those he healed, not the disciples, and finally not even the women prove faithful and speak the word of promise—the good news—of which Mark's story marks a "beginning." But the last verses do offer a promise: "There you will see him, just as he told you." The promise rests with the one who made it and his ability to keep his word. Is that one to be trusted, even while others fail? Such a question presumes that the Jesus whom the tomb cannot hold, and the God who raised him from the dead, are realities among those who experience the Gospel on this side of the text.

The question of God's faithfulness and reliability is something that can tie the story together from beginning to end. Is there reason to believe that Jesus can redeem—that he is one who on God's behalf can forgive sins and liberate those in bondage? Such confidence will arise not only from the testimony of the demons and of God, but from confidence that God keeps promises. Jesus' predictions have an important function in the story. John the Baptist promises that the "stronger one" will baptize with the Holy Spirit. The parables promise that despite the apparent waste, the sower will reap a great harvest. Tiny seeds will produce great shrubs. What is hidden will be revealed, and the words will give life. Troubles ahead are only birth pangs, anticipating the dawning of a new time when the elect will be gathered from the four corners of the earth.

While on the one hand the story is full of promises yet to be kept at the story's end, on the other hand many are fulfilled within the context of the narrative. Jesus predicts his death and resurrection in detail. He goes "as it has been written of him." Peter denies Jesus three times before the second crow of the cock, while Jesus is being taunted as a prophet. The disciples flee, precisely as Jesus said. He dies, and early in the morning the women find the tomb empty—as he said. The story ends with one final promise, "as he told you."

For those who imagine that a successful ending is available to interpreters as some kind of achievement, the ending will be disappointing, even crushing. The women finally fail, as do the disciples and everyone else. All that is left is a promise—a promise made by the one whom God raised from the dead. How that promise will be kept is not spelled out. That the women relented and told the disciples, and that they went to Galilee and met Jesus—none of this is said. But the story has a future. As Jesus could not be confined in the tomb, so the promises cannot be contained within the story.

So long as God is not the main actor in the story, and so long as the reality of God is excluded from the world of the actual reader, the narrative is bound to disappoint. If the story is to become "good news" to anyone, it will depend upon God's work beyond the ending of Mark's story. The matter reaches to the heart of engagement with the New Testament.

CHAPTER 10

SECRETS AND SECRECY

A feature of Mark's Gospel, made famous by Wilhelm Wrede's *The Messianic Secret in the Gospels,* written around the turn of the century, is the secrecy that enshrouds Jesus' ministry—a self-imposed secrecy. The theme is introduced early in the story:

> And [he] cast out many demons; and he would not permit the demons to speak, because they knew him. (Mark 1:34)

> Whenever the unclean spirits saw him, they fell down before him and shouted, "You are the Son of God!" But he sternly ordered them not to make him known. (3:11-12)

Several things are notable. The first is that demons and unclean spirits, as supernatural beings, know from the outset who Jesus is: they acknowledge him as the "Holy One of God" (1:24), "the Son of God" (3:11), "the Son of the Most High God" (5:7). No human beings in the story use the terms prior to the passion narrative, and then they are used by Jesus' adversaries who have no idea the titles may be appropriate. Second is that Jesus silences the spirits not because they are saying things that are untrue but because they are speaking the truth about him. Why that is inappropriate we shall have to learn. Finally, while others are presumably present at these encounters with unclean spirits, the supernatural testimony to Jesus' identity as "Son of God" makes no impact on the audience. There is no "uptake," to use a term from J. L. Austin.[1] No one in the story takes up the language. When Jesus asks his followers who people believe him to be (Mark 8:27), they do not include "the Son of God" among the titles. The only audience to benefit from the comments by the narrator is the reader of the Gospel. That is no small matter. If Jesus' identity is a "secret," it is not so for readers of Mark who are told from the outset who Jesus is and hear heavenly declarations and the supernatural testimony of the spirits.

That secrecy focuses on Jesus' identity is likewise highlighted in the account of Peter's confession, long recognized as a turning point or "hinge" in the narrative:

> Jesus went on with his disciples to the villages of Caesarea Philippi; and on the way he asked his disciples, "Who do people say that I am?" And they answered him, "John the Baptist; and others, Elijah; and still others, one of the prophets." He asked them, "But who do you say that I am?" Peter answered him, "You are the Messiah." And he sternly ordered them not to tell anyone about him.
>
> (Mark 8:27-30)

That Jesus' identity as Messiah (Christ) is to be kept secret has led to identifying the mystery as "the messianic secret."

Another feature of the secrecy motif is Jesus' frequent enjoining to silence those whom he heals. Nothing specific is said about his identity in these passages.

> [And he said] to him, "See that you say nothing to anyone; but go, show yourself to the priest, and offer for your cleansing what Moses commanded, as a testimony to them." (Mark 1:44)

> And immediately the girl got up and began to walk about (she was twelve years of age). At this they were overcome with amazement. He strictly ordered them that no one should know this. (5:42-43)

> And immediately his ears were opened, his tongue was released, and he spoke plainly. Then Jesus ordered them to tell no one.
>
> (7:35-36)

Sometimes these injunctions are followed by a comment that people did not do as they were told.

> But he went out and began to proclaim it freely, and to spread the word, so that Jesus could no longer go into a town openly, but stayed out in the country; and people came to him from every quarter. (1:45)

> But the more he ordered them, the more zealously they proclaimed it. (7:36)

One reason for attention to these injunctions to silence is that they do not make good sense. Jesus' purpose cannot be to remain hidden; his ministry is public. It is likewise clearly stated that he gathers followers to make the good news known:

> And he appointed twelve, whom he also named apostles, to be with him, and to be sent out to proclaim the message, and to have authority to cast out demons. (3:14-15)[2]

What the secrecy motif has to do with the public ministry for which the disciples are chosen is not immediately obvious.

Still another feature of the secrecy is Jesus' intentional concealment of his message from "outsiders." Chapter 3 gives some sense of Jesus' relationship to various groups that surround him. There are the religious authorities, who are suspicious; his family, who believe him to be out of his mind; the crowds who flock to him; and a special group of disciples, at the center of which are the twelve whom Jesus chooses to be with him. The world drawn by the narrative is made up of concentric circles: There are insiders and outsiders. That apparently is what Jesus intends. When his disciples ask him about the meaning of the parables, he says:

> To you has been given the secret of the kingdom of God, but for those outside, everything comes in parables, in order that they may indeed look, but not perceive, and may indeed listen, but not understand; so that they may not turn again and be forgiven.
> (Mark 4:11-12)

The "secret of the kingdom of God" is not defined. Particularly because the phrase appears in the context of agricultural stories

Jesus tells to shed light on "the kingdom of God," there is little justification for understanding the phrase exclusively in christological terms. There may be more to the secrecy, in other words, than Jesus' identity. Precisely what the secret constitutes, however, is left unspecified.

The difficult words have caught the attention of more than one commentator. They appear in a softened and expanded form in Matthew's version of the parable of the sower (Matt 13:10-17), and even these words are simply omitted from the version of the parable appointed to be read in churches in the major lectionaries. To say there is a conspiracy to silence Mark at this point would be only a slight exaggeration. Parable interpreters have sought every method at their disposal to dismiss the words. There is some irony in the flight from their clear meaning: Jesus says he conceals in order to harden his audience, and it seems to work. Most who read these words are hardened.

It is likewise clear that Jesus' obscurity is a strategy. In the words following Jesus' explanation of the parable of the sower, he says,

> Is a lamp brought in to be put under the bushel basket, or under the bed, and not on the lampstand? For there is nothing hidden, except to be disclosed; nor is anything secret, except to come to light. (4:21-22)

Secrecy is apparently provisional, part of a program that will end with openness and clarity. No explanation is offered, and the kind of psychological speculation typical of popular Jesus books does not provide satisfying answers. We learn only that the time of openness will come. The obvious question is, When will it come? The Gospel offers clues. On the way down from the Mount of Transfiguration, Jesus charges his disciples to keep what has happened to themselves:

> As they were coming down the mountain, he ordered them to tell no one about what they had seen, until after the Son of Man had risen from the dead. (9:9)

The disciples have no idea what Jesus is talking about, but for the reader at least there seems to be emerging a strategy: Jesus' resurrection, it seems, will mark the beginning of a new chapter.

The time when those whom Jesus has chosen will proclaim the good news openly will be after the Resurrection. And Jesus promises that such a time will come:

> And the good news must first be proclaimed to all nations. When they bring you to trial and hand you over, do not worry beforehand about what you are to say; but say whatever is given you at that time, for it is not you who speak, but the Holy Spirit. (13:10-11)

Finally, Jesus anticipates an even greater end to secrecy, perhaps we could say *the* end:

> But in those days, after that suffering, the sun will be darkened, and the moon will not give its light, and the stars will be falling from heaven, and the powers in the heavens will be shaken. Then they will see "the Son of Man coming in clouds" with great power and glory. (Mark 13:24-26)

Several questions remain for interpreting the narrative. One has to do with temporal questions: When will the time of openness come? The question becomes all the more urgent in light of the disappointing ending: When in the face of an empty tomb, women are commanded to speak, they do not (16:8). We shall have to ask what it means that the Gospel ends with Jesus still enshrouded in mystery and characters still in the dark.

Another question has to do with the singling out of the disciples as insiders. Jesus gives them explanations when others get only riddles. Will they understand the secret of the kingdom of God? Will they finally be able to give their witness?

Finally, we might ask why it is so difficult to understand Jesus and what he is about. What is complex about the story?

UNSEEING EYES, UNHEARING EARS, HARDENED HEARTS

Scholars have proposed a variety of solutions to the problem of secrecy. Some depend upon reconstructing the situation behind the composition of the Gospel. The problem may be approached historically, for example. Did Jesus try to keep his identity a secret? Did he realize that it would be too dangerous for information to leak out—that people would misunderstand "Messiah" in political terms? Answering the question would presume a great deal. It must assume we can know what "the Messiah" would have meant to Jesus and his followers and that we have access to Jesus' notions about himself (his "messianic self-consciousness," to use the technical term). The dearth of information about Jesus' self-reflection in Mark means reading Jesus' mind is almost pure speculation, depending finally upon inaccessible information. And even if such information were available, such interpretation deals with Mark's story by explaining it (or explaining it away).

An alternative is to deal with pre-Markan tradition. In his famous book on the "Messianic Secret," Wrede argued that the "secret" is a literary construct that derives from tradition prior to Mark. That Jesus kept his identity hidden is a way of explaining why people did not recognize Jesus as the Messiah during his lifetime. Like others of his colleagues, Wrede presumed that the confession of Jesus as "Messiah" was not the only evaluation of Jesus and that in fact those who connected and handed on stories about Jesus' miracles and accounts of his teaching did not think of him as Messiah at all. The so-called Q source, for example, a hypothetical collection of Jesus' teachings that seems to have circulated without a narrative context, did not speak of Jesus as "Messiah." He is pictured as a sage. Those who collected stories about Jesus' miracles may have pictured him as a prophet. The Gospels, in this view, enlist the nonmessianic tradition about Jesus—accounts of his teaching and healing—in service of proclaiming Jesus the Christ and eventually in telling the story of the preached Christ. Wrede was convinced that the secrecy motif was not historical—that is, it did not go back to Jesus—but could be explained through understanding the development of tradition. The "secret" was the device by which the two traditions about Jesus could be connected: Jesus is the Messiah, but he was not recognized as such during his lifetime because he kept it hidden.

Wrede's account is no less speculative than that of those who seek to explain Mark by appeal to the historical Jesus, though there is at least evidence of different forms of tradition about Jesus in Paul's letters and in noncanonical writings. Even here, however, such "explanations" do not suffice if we agree that the narrative has importance beyond what it signifies. If the story itself is a reality to be dealt with—and if the story intends to move its readers—explaining the text based on what lies behind it is insufficient. Interpreters must ask how "secrecy" works as a feature of the story—or, to use the language of Frank Kermode, what we are to make of it as a property of narrative. If we have reason to believe that Mark's Gospel is more than a thoughtless collection of material, interpretation must include some estimate of the impact of the "secret" and secrecy on an experience of the story.

Interpretations of Mark 4:10-12 provide a particularly striking example of strategies that do not take the present text of Mark seriously. Source critics can find reasons to suspect that the "explanation" of parables did not always follow the parable of the sower. In the simpler version of the parable in the *Gospel of Thomas,* there is no explanation. There is evidence even within the Gospels themselves for regarding the "explanation" as an addition to the parable during the history of transmission. The scene shifts, for one thing. At one moment Jesus is in a boat speaking to a crowd; suddenly he is "alone" with an inside group. And they ask about "the parables," while thus far Jesus has told only one. That the verses might at some point have been appended to the "original" parable may suggest another context in which the verses might be studied—not their present setting within the Gospel of Mark but within oral tradition.

Joachim Jeremias, whose work on the parables we have noted earlier, pursues this line of argument.[3] He suggests that the parables should be read as authentic words of Jesus. He is even willing to regard the saying about insiders and outsiders as Jesus' own words, but spoken originally in another setting. Retranslating Mark's Greek into Aramaic, the language Jesus spoke, Jeremias identifies what he believes must have been a translation error in 4:12: Jesus must have said people would not understand "unless" they turned and were forgiven. Recognizing the mistake, interpreters are free to understand the statement "so that they may not turn again and be forgiven" as meaning "unless they repent and be forgiven."

Even apart from Jeremias's unconvincing reconstruction, what is remarkable is that an intelligent interpreter simply refuses to deal with the present text of Mark's Gospel, according to which Jesus tells riddles so that people will not understand and will not repent. The possibility of a mistranslation of Aramaic provides an

183

excuse for ignoring Mark's Greek. Commentators who regularly speak of the verses as "Mark's Parable Theory" likewise refuse to take the passage seriously. Unless one chooses to read another book, there must be some accounting for the genuine horror the verse elicits from readers. From the perspective of Jesus' character in Mark's Gospel, why would Jesus say (and do) such a thing with regard to outsiders? Any explanation, if there is one, must be sought first within the narrative argument. And if Jesus' statement makes use of images from Isaiah 6, interpretation can include some attention to this famous passage, the history of its interpretation, and its use in Mark. That God hardens is a theme familiar from Israel's scriptures, well developed in the Fourth Gospel and in Paul's letter to the Romans. How it functions rhetorically in Mark's Gospel is one of the more significant questions for interpreters. Does Jesus, acting on God's behalf, consciously harden hearers so that they will not understand? Does he have that power? And if so, how will it be used?

A TEST CASE: THE DISCIPLES

A host of interpreters have identified discipleship as a major theme in Mark. The earliest Gospel is certainly more interested in the disciples than in outsiders, from whom little can be expected. The singling out of the disciples and the repeated mention of their presence (or of an inner circle) suggest that the story of Jesus' ministry is also about the followers he selected. And in view of the promises Jesus makes to them, it should likewise be clear that if there is to be a continuation of this story, the twelve will have a major role to play.

Troubling, then, is the repeated emphasis on the disciples' failure to understand. Their inability to grasp who Jesus is and what he is up to is highlighted by three boat scenes. The first occurs just after Jesus has explained parables to them. Crossing the lake, they are caught in a storm. They awaken Jesus, terrified. He calms the storm, then turns to his followers:

> He said to them, "Why are you afraid? Have you still no faith?" And they were filled with great awe and said to one another, "Who then is this, that even the wind and the sea obey him?" (4:40-41)

184

The dramatic scene is followed by some of the most spectacular miracles in the Gospel. Jesus casts out a legion of demons, cures a woman of a hemorrhage, and brings back to life the daughter of Jairus, the ruler of a synagogue. Of these wonders the disciples, at least the inner circle, are witnesses. The disciples are then sent out on their own, to preach and heal (6:6-13). When they return, they try to withdraw to a deserted place to rest but are followed by crowds, whom Jesus feeds miraculously with five loaves and two fish. Afterward, the disciples set out for the other side in a boat, leaving Jesus behind to pray. In the evening, they see Jesus walking toward them on the water, and they are terrified.

> But when they saw him walking on the sea, they thought it was a ghost and cried out; for they all saw him and were terrified. But immediately he spoke to them and said, "Take heart, it is I; do not be afraid." Then he got into the boat with them and the wind ceased. And they were utterly astounded, for they did not understand about the loaves, but *their hearts were hardened.* (6:49-52, emphasis added)

There follows another series of miracles, including another miraculous feeding of a large crowd. Once again the disciples set out by boat. This time Jesus is with them, and they have a confused conversation with him about bread.

> Jesus said to them, "Why are you talking about having no bread? Do you still not perceive or understand? *Are your hearts hardened? Do you have eyes, and fail to see? Do you have ears, and fail to hear?* And do you not remember? When I broke the five loaves for the five thousand, how many baskets full of pieces did you collect?" They said to him, "Twelve." "And the seven for the four thousand, how many baskets full of broken pieces did you collect?" And they said to him, "Seven." Then he said to them, "Do you not yet understand?" (8:17-21, emphasis added)

The disciples, who have been present throughout, not only witnessing Jesus' miracles and teaching but receiving special instruction, seem no different from outsiders. Having eyes, they do not see; having ears, they do not hear (8:18). But why? What reasons are given for their lack of understanding? One is offered in the words of the narrator: "They did not understand about the loaves, but their hearts were hardened" (6:52). The verb is passive, with God as the implied subject. In light of OT precedent, it suggests that something has been done to them. Elaborate psychological interpretations of the image, suggesting that they have somehow hardened themselves, simply ignore the imagery. If the purpose of the narrative were to ridicule the disciples or to use them as negative examples, other imagery would have been more appropriate. Blindness and deafness and hardness of heart are images that do not lend themselves to moral exhortation. If the problem of the disciples—and all those who do not understand—is that they are blind, the solution to their problem will not come through reprimand or education or encouragement. They will require healing. If, like the demoniacs, they are bound by a power beyond themselves, someone will have to set them free. The question of the story, then, is whether that occurs. If it does not—if the story leaves the disciples bound and blind, it is difficult to imagine how this can be good news to anyone.

A great deal is at stake here—in fact, nothing less than the possibility of experiencing the story as good news. Suggesting that the disciples serve as foils for "ideal readers" simply ignores the depth of the problem. If sight and insight are gifts of God, there must be some reason to imagine God will open eyes and ears, most especially in the case of those whom Jesus has chosen. For if God abandons the disciples to their blindness, there is no reason to imagine God will enlighten any particular readers who lack the ability to glimpse the truth. Interpretation does not solve the problem but only indicates how much is at stake. Does God give sight to the blind? Will God give sight to those who cannot see or hear the truth?

SIGHT TO THE BLIND

There are two crucial accounts of the healing of the blind in the narrative. The first is perhaps the more interesting. In the unusual story, which follows without transition the scene in which Jesus confronts his disciples with their own blindness, Jesus heals a blind man, but in two stages.

He took the blind man by the hand and led him out of the village; and when he had put saliva on his eyes and laid his hands on him, he asked him, "Can you see anything?" And the man looked up and said, "I can see people, but they look like trees, walking." Then Jesus laid his hands on his eyes again; and he looked intently and his sight was restored, and he saw everything clearly. (8:23-25)

The form of the story is without precedent in tales of the wondrous. It seems to suggest that the hero did not have the power to get a healing right on the first try. Some kind of figurative reading seems required. It is also near at hand. The disciples have just demonstrated that they are still blind to the secrets of Jesus' mission. Then follows the story of Jesus' healing of a blind man who, at first, sees, but dimly. What follows is an account of the first apparent breakthrough for the disciples.

And on the way he asked his disciples, "Who do people say that I am?" And they answered him, "John the Baptist; and others, Elijah; and still others, one of the prophets." He asked them, "But who do you say that I am?" Peter answered him, "You are the Messiah." And he *sternly ordered* them that they not tell anyone about him.

Then he began to teach them that the Son of Man must undergo great suffering, and be rejected by the elders, the chief priests, and the scribes, and be killed, and after three days rise again. He said all this quite openly. And Peter took him aside and began to *rebuke* him. But turning and looking at his disciples, he *rebuked* Peter and said, "Get behind me, Satan! For you are setting your mind not on divine things but on human things." (8:27-33, emphasis added)

Translation of the passage is difficult. The term translated "sternly ordered" is the same as the one translated "rebuke" in the following verses: Peter rebukes Jesus and Jesus rebukes Peter (8:32, 33). It is also the term used to speak of Jesus' "rebuking" of the wind and the sea (4:39) and his rebuke of demons (1:25; 3:12; 9:25). The term seems to have a negative tone, not adequately captured in "sternly ordered."

What does Jesus' response mean? That Peter has made a good confession we know from elsewhere in the Gospel (1:1; 14:62), but that Jesus is "the Christ" is not apparent from anything in his ministry, which seems to suggest he is a prophet (see chapter 4, pp. 98ff., on titles and messianic expectations in first-century Judaism). But perhaps there is something more. Peter anticipates what is to come, saying something genuinely new: perhaps as "the Christ," Jesus will take power and reign. Jesus' "rebuke" does not necessarily mean Peter is wrong. Jesus rebukes the demons and unclean spirits when they speak the truth before its time. The same is apparently true of Peter and the Twelve.

That Peter does not understand what he says becomes immediately clear in what follows. Jesus predicts what lies ahead: he will be rejected, killed, and after three days rise (8:31). In view of his forecast, Peter "rebukes" him. Such defeat has no place in expectations of the Messiah-King who is to come. If Jesus is the one who will "slay the wicked with the breath of his mouth" and inherit David's throne forever, there is no place for the future Jesus announces for himself. Peter balks. And Jesus then rebukes Peter: "Get behind me, Satan!" he says. "For you are setting your mind not on divine things but on human things" (8:33).

Peter is not wrong in his statement about Jesus. The words are correct; Jesus is the Christ. But Peter has no sense of what his "confession" means. The words will sound quite different in light of the death and vindication of "the Christ, the Son of the Blessed One," and "King of the Jews." There is no reason Peter should understand, at least based on Jewish scriptural tradition. And if there is a great chasm between "God's things" and "human things," coming to understand the difference may entail something like a death, to use imagery familiar from Paul's letter to the Romans. That Peter has the words right may mean little more than it means for those possessed by unclean spirits to acknowledge Jesus' identity. He at last has the words, but will he ever come to understand them? Will he ever glimpse "God's ways" as opposed to "human ways"?

The story of the blind man seems to offer some promise. Jesus heals those who are blind and cannot open their own eyes. Jesus' cure, however, works only partially the first time for the man in Bethsaida. Jesus must touch the eyes of the blind man for a second time, after which he sees everything clearly. Perhaps the same will be true for Peter and the disciples. They have glimpsed the truth, but still unclearly. Perhaps Jesus will finally touch them so that they can see and hear and speak. Without such a touch, there is no reason to imagine an escape from the darkness of "human ways." The story, about mystery and concealment, promises openness and enlightenment, just as it promises that what is sown will bear fruit. The question remains: When?

IMPLIED READERS AND ACTUAL READERS

As the story ends, numerous questions remain to be answered for actual readers. They cover a broad range, from informational (Exactly what did the disciples do after they ran away? How was their faith in Jesus reborn? What happened to Judas? Did the women tell the disciples finally, and did they meet Jesus in Galilee? Did Jesus actually appear to Peter, and what was the nature of the encounter? Who is the young man who ran away naked when Jesus was arrested?) to more theological (What is the kingdom of God? Precisely how are Jesus' predictions in chapter thirteen related to the real future?). Is the story true?

Part of the experience of mystification may be attributed to cultural and historical distances: there are aspects of Mark's world unfamiliar to us. Reconstructing that world may help. Some of the questions would have been answered for those who knew the story of the early church—who knew, for example, that Jesus "appeared to Cephas, then to the twelve, then . . . to more than five hundred brothers and sisters" (1 Cor 15:5-7). Just as understanding Jewish purity laws can make sense of controversies as well as the peculiar behavior of the woman who must come up behind Jesus to touch his robe (5:27-28), so Jesus' strange statements to the Zebedees about "drinking the cup" and undergoing a baptism (10:38) make more sense when read in light of traditions about the Lord's Supper (1 Cor 11:17-32) and Baptism (Rom 6:1-5) known to be part of tradition prior to Paul. We can never know, of course, precisely what the author expects of implied readers, but study can enrich the experience of hearing.

There is little likelihood, however, that more information will settle all questions and make the reading experience satisfying. Interpretations of Mark continue to proliferate as the Gospel seems to gain in popularity, suggesting there is something about Mark's narrative that resists capture. On the one hand, readers are constructed as insiders ("constructed" because it is not a matter about which readers have a choice). We know what characters in the story do not and cannot. We hear voices, are made aware of biblical associations, are given clues unavailable to those in the story. Yet something always remains beyond the reader's grasp.

There is a sense in which the Gospel resists closure at its deepest level. Mark's work is unlike modern stories that intend to disappoint and frustrate; it is, after all, a promising story. The experience of reading, however, is not satisfying. Those who imagine that interpretation will finally rein in the story and force it to yield its secrets will experience disappointment. For such interpreters, reading with Frank Kermode is a salutary experience. An encounter with Mark, he argues, suggests that the story is finally not about secrets but secrecy.[4] However particular questions are answered, at the end readers are left without the means to control interpretation. Jesus is not at hand, to be grasped or fixed or interrogated. So-called insiders are finally left without the means to guarantee that they have a place in the Kingdom or that the story is good news for them. They may be poor soil or rocky soil. And the one who determines such matters, who opens eyes and ears, is not within the control of interpreters. In such a situation, interpretation will not solve the "problem" of the reader; it will not satisfy the need for an ending.

A regular response is to turn to the other Gospels or Acts for a more satisfying experience. In Matthew the women actually take hold of Jesus' feet as he meets them after their visit to the empty tomb (Matt 28:9). In Luke-Acts, the disciples not only see Jesus but spend forty days with him after the Resurrection (Acts 1:3). In the Gospel of John, Thomas is invited to place his fingers in the nail holes and his hand in the spear wound in Jesus' side (John 20:27). Resort to other Gospels is not a reading of Mark, however—and in any case, none of the Gospels provides the kind of closure that constitutes a genuine "ending." Readers are to be aware that Jesus is gone, no longer available. The point is well made in John, where Jesus says to Thomas: "Have you believed because you have seen me? Blessed are those who have not seen and yet have come to believe" (20:29). The only thing left is a word. Words have power but not substance. They disappear when spoken and must thus be spoken again and again.

If Mark's Gospel is not unique in refusing to provide readers with a genuine ending, it is perhaps the most unrelenting in undermining confidence in anything but trust in the work of God beyond the confines of the story. Readers are left with silent women and a story still enshrouded in mystery—and a host of promises. We are surely to imagine that some of the promises will be kept. Jesus will meet the disciples, and they will continue the work for which they have been chosen. The story will be told, the clearest proof of which is the Gospel itself. Yet crucial promises remain outstanding, most especially the promises intended for actual readers. If the story proves to be good news for any particular reader, it will not be because interpretive cunning or violence permit readers to lay hold of Jesus and confine him long enough to extract a blessing. "He is not here," the young man says.

Yet that elusiveness also means that the story does not allow for negative closure either. The story ends with promises as well as disappointment: "there you will see him, just as he told you." There is only an empty tomb, the stone rolled back to reveal that Jesus cannot be held even by death. The presence of the liberator remains a possibility against which interpretation can offer no sure defense. There is still the possibility that Jesus will come to give sight to particular blind persons and that there will be a day when "all will see." Only under those circumstances can there be a genuine resolving of the "messianic secret." But will such a thing occur? That, of course, remains to be seen.

There is an old debate about whether the Bible can be interpreted properly only by believers or if interpretation is open to everyone. On the one hand, the answer is obvious. Anyone can read and interpret the Bible. It is a public book. When it comes to deciding upon a Greek text or translating a phrase or making an historical assessment, there are no special advantages that accrue to believers. The debate, however, may point in a different direction. If the Gospel story argues that there are matters on which everything rests—like the ability to distinguish between "God's things" and "human things"—and that we lack the power to discern them apart from a healing touch or a liberating word, the difference between reading done within the context of a believing or an unbelieving community may have a great deal to do with the impact of the story. Only if Jesus is alive and active beyond the confines of the story—and only if Jesus acts on particular people in the present—can the Gospel story be experienced as the beginning of the good news. If Jesus is absent and God is silent, Mark's Gospel can only be experienced as disappointing and unsettling. And if this is the case, it is not surprising that interpretation will seek to distance the work and protect contemporary readers from that unsatisfying experience.

At stake is not so much the "meaning" of Mark's Gospel as its impact on hearers. And on this matter, the testimony of believers who have read the Gospel as part of the scriptures within the context of a worshiping community is that God does continue to work beyond the confines of the story—and that the continuing work of God is the "one thing necessary" for those who read the Gospel.

NOTES

INTRODUCTION: INTERPRETING MARK'S GOSPEL

1. My translation. Alternative translations can be found in almost any introductory text or commentary on Mark. The "Testimony of Papias" is found in Eusebius, *hist. eccl.* III, 39, 1-7.14-17.
2. The suggestion was made in an important and little-read article by Joseph Kuerzinger published in a collection of essays honoring Rudolf Bultmann in the 1950s, the latest version of which is "Die Aussage des Papias von Hierapolis zur literarischen Form des Markusevangeliums" ["The statement of Papias of Hierapolis on the literary form of Mark's Gospel"], *BZ* 21 (1977): 245-64; for a discussion of his proposal, see my *Master of Surprise: Mark Interpreted* (Minneapolis: Fortress Press, 1994), 12-13.
3. Martin Dibelius, *From Tradition to Gospel,* trans. B. L. Woolf (New York: Scribners, 1956), 3.
4. W. Wrede, *The Messianic Secret,* trans. J. C. G. Grieg (Cambridge: James Clarke, 1971).
5. For a helpful discussion of the alternatives, see the article by Patrick Keifert, "Mind-Reader and Maestro: Models for Understanding Biblical Interpreters," *Word and World* 1 (1981): 153-68.
6. K. L. Schmidt, *Der Rahmen der Geschichte Jesu* [The Framework of the Story of Jesus] (Berlin: Trowitzsch & Sohn, 1919; reprinted by the Wissenschaftliche Buchgesellschaft, 1969).
7. Willi Marxsen, *Mark the Evangelist,* trans. D. Juel et al. (Nashville/New York: Abingdon Press, 1969).
8. Kenneth R. R. Gros-Louis, *Literary Interpretation of Biblical Narratives* (Nashville/New York: Abingdon Press, 1974).
9. Frank Kermode, *The Genesis of Secrecy: On the Interpretation of Narrative* (Cambridge, Mass.: Harvard University Press, 1979); coed., *The Literary Guide to the Bible* (Cambridge, Mass.: Harvard University Press, 1987).
10. Norman Perrin, *What Is Redaction Criticism?* (Philadelphia: Fortress Press, 1969), 42.

11. For a critique of the source-critical preoccupation, see Juel, *Messiah and Temple: The Trial of Jesus in the Gospel of Mark*, SBLDS 31 (Missoula, Mont.: Scholars Press, 1977), 25-29.

12. Robert Tannehill, "The Disciples in Mark: The Function of a Narrative Role," *JR* 57 (1977): 386-405. See also his two-volume *The Narrative Unity of Luke-Acts* (Minneapolis: Fortress Press, 1986–1990), an experiment with the form of commentary appropriate to narrative.

13. Ernest Best, *Following Jesus: Discipleship in the Gospel of Mark* (Sheffield: JSOT Press, 1981).

14. Juel, *Messiah and Temple;* John Donahue, *Are You the Christ? The Trial Narrative in the Gospel of Mark*, SBLDS 10 (Missoula, Mont.: Scholars Press, 1973); and Frank Matera, *The Kingship of Jesus*, SBLDS 66 (Chico, Calif.: Scholars Press, 1982).

15. David Rhoads and Donald Michie, *Mark as Story: An Introduction to the Narrative of a Gospel* (Philadelphia: Fortress Press, 1982).

16. Mary Ann Tolbert, *Sowing the Gospel: Mark's World in Literary-Historical Perspective* (Minneapolis: Fortress Press, 1989).

17. John Donahue, *The Gospel as Parable* (Philadelphia: Fortress Press, 1988).

18. Stanley Fish, *Is There a Text in This Class?* (Cambridge, Mass.: Harvard University Press, 1980).

19. Robert Fowler, *Let the Reader Understand: Reader Response Criticism and the Gospel of Mark* (Minneapolis: Fortress Press, 1991), 9.

20. See, e.g., Howard Clark Kee, *Community of the New Age: Studies in Mark's Gospel* (Philadelphia: Westminster, 1977).

21. Albert Schweitzer, *The Quest of the Historical Jesus,* trans. W. Montgomery (New York: Macmillan, 1961), 360.

22. See the comments in Fowler, *Let the Reader Understand,* 10-11.

23. See Eric Auerbach, *Mimesis,* trans. W. R. Trask (Princeton, N.J.: Princeton University Press, 1953).

24. See Barnabas Lindars, *Jesus Son of Man* (Grand Rapids: Wm. B. Eerdmans Publishing Co.; London: SPCK, 1983); Douglas Hare, *The Son of Man Tradition* (Minneapolis: Fortress Press, 1990); and Donald Juel, *Messianic Exegesis: Christological Interpretation of the Old Testament in Early Christianity* (Philadelphia: Fortress Press, 1988), chap. 7.

25. Harry Gamble, *Books and Readers in the Early Church: A History of Early Christian Texts* (New Haven: Yale University Press, 1995).

1. THE OPENING

1. Translation of 1:4 as it appears in the most recent edition of the Greek New Testament should read, "John the baptizer appeared in the wilderness *and* preaching a baptism of repentance for the forgiveness of sins." Other Greek versions solve the problem by reading "John appeared baptizing and preaching" or "John the baptizer appeared ... preaching" (the reading apparently favored by the translators of the NRSV).

2. Josephus describes John in *Antiquities* XVIII.116-19.
3. While the text of the Old Testament that appears in English Bibles is translated from the Hebrew, the order of books is not that of the Hebrew Bible but of the Greek Old Testament. New Testament writers and their communities spoke and read Greek. Their Bible was the Greek translation of the Jewish Bible known as the Septuagint.
4. One of the most interesting books that recounts traditional interpretations of the story of Abraham and Isaac is Shalom Spiegel's *The Last Trial*, trans. Judah Goldin (New York: Shocken Books, 1969).

2. THE PLAYERS

1. For further information on the various "sects" or parties within Judaism, see standard reference works like E. Schurer, *The History of the Jewish People in the Age of Jesus Christ*, rev. and ed. G. Vermes, F. Millar, and M. Black (Edinburgh: T. and T. Clark, 1973–87).
2. The first to call attention to the various official identifications was Paul Winter, *On the Trial of Jesus* (Berlin: Gruyter, 1961). See also Ellis Rivkin, *What Crucified Jesus?* (Nashville: Abingdon Press, 1984); and E. P. Sanders, *Judaism: Practice and Belief, 63 BCE–66 CE* (Philadelphia: Trinity Press International, 1992).
3. For a thorough discussion of all problems relating to the trial and death of Jesus, the best resource is now the monumental work by Raymond Brown, *The Death of the Messiah* (New York: Doubleday, 1994).
4. Elisabeth Schüssler Fiorenza, *In Memory of Her: A Feminist Theological Reconstruction of Christian Origins* (New York: Crossroad, 1983), 42.

3. WHO IS GOD?

1. Some ancient manuscripts omit "Son of God" in Mark 1:1. The evidence is so evenly divided that the official committees cannot make up their minds. We will read "Son of God" as part of the text, with the NRSV and the 27th ed. of the standard Greek New Testament. In the 28th ed., however, "Son of God" will be placed in the notes and not in the text.

4. WHO IS JESUS?

1. A variety of accessible and helpful essays is included in the volume by W. S. Green, *Approaches to Ancient Judaism: Theory and Practice* Brown Judaism Studies 1 (Missoula, Mont.: Scholars Press, 1978); also helpful is Rowan Greer and James Kugel, *Early Biblical Interpretation* (Philadelphia: Westminster, 1986). See also chap. 2 of *Messianic Exegesis.*
2. For a comprehensive survey of contemporary scholarship on this issue, see James Charlesworth, ed., *The Messiah: Developments in Earliest Judaism and Christianity* (Philadelphia: Fortress Press, 1992).

3. For further discussion of eschatological figures in the Dead Sea Scrolls, see Juel, *Messianic Exegesis*, 61-77.

5. PLUNDERING SATAN'S HOUSE

1. The most compelling account of Mark as a political argument is Ched Myers, *Binding the Strong Man* (Maryknoll, N.Y.: Orbis Books, 1988).
2. Schweitzer, *Quest of the Historical Jesus*, 330-97.

6. THE TEACHER

1. This is the argument of Joachim Jeremias in his very influential book, *The Parables of Jesus*, trans. S. H. Hooke (New York: Scribners, 1962).
2. *Gospel of Thomas*, saying 9. The translation is from Kurt Aland, *Synopsis Quattuor Evangeliorum* (Stuttgart: Württembergische Bibelanstalt, 1964), 518.
3. Jeremias, *Parables of Jesus*.
4. Kermode, *Genesis of Secrecy*, chap. 2.
5. Meir Sternberg, *The Poetics of Biblical Narrative: Ideological Literature and the Drama of Reading* (Bloomington, Ind.: Indiana University Press, 1985), 48-49. See Juel, *Master of Surprise*, chap. 4, for a discussion of their views.

7. THE DEATH OF THE KING

1. See Juel, *Messiah and Temple*.
2. Raymond Brown, *The Death of the Messiah*, Anchor Bible Reference Library (New York: Doubleday, 1994).
3. James Charlesworth, ed., *The Messiah: Developments in Earliest Judaism and Christianity* (Minneapolis: Fortress Press, 1992).

8. THE DEATH OF JESUS AND THE WILL OF GOD

1. For an insightful review of various atonement theories as well as an important constructive proposal, see Gerhard Forde, "The Work of Christ" in *Christian Dogmatics* (ed. R. Jenson and C. Braaten; Philadelphia: Fortress Press, 1984).
2. For an English translation, see Anselm of Canterbury, *Why God Became Man* (Albany, N.Y.: Magi Books, 1969).
3. C. S. Lewis, *The Lion, the Witch, and the Wardrobe: A Children's Story* (New York: Collier, 1970).
4. Ibid., 138-40.
5. Ibid., 152.
6. Ibid., 159-60.

9. ENDINGS AND BEGINNINGS

1. For a brief but helpful discussion of the various endings, see Kurt and Barbara Aland, *The Text of the New Testament*, trans. E. Rhodes (Grand

Rapids: Wm. B. Eerdmans Publishing Co., 1987), 292-93.
2. On the matter of endings, see the work by Frank Kermode, *The Sense of an Ending: Studies in the Theory of Fiction* (London: Oxford University Press, 1966), and *Genesis of Secrecy,* esp. the last chapter.
3. For a helpful discussion of such matters, see the fine article by Andrew Lincoln, "The Promise and the Failure—Mark 16:7, 8," *JBL* 108 (1989): 283-300.
4. Robert Tannehill, "Disciples," 404.
5. Fowler, *Let the Reader Understand,* 250.
6. Kermode, *Genesis of Secrecy,* 125-45.

10. SECRETS AND SECRECY

1. Cited in Fowler, *Let the Reader Understand,* 18.
2. See Tannehill, "The Disciples in Mark: The Function of a Narrative Role" *JR* 57 (1977): 386-405.
3. See above, chap. 6, on Jeremias's argument in *The Parables of Jesus.*
4. Kermode, *Genesis of Secrecy,* 143-45.

BIBLIOGRAPHY

Black, Clifton. *Mark: Images of an Apostolic Interpreter.* Columbia: University of South Carolina Press, 1994.

Blount, Brian. *Cultural Interpretation: Reorienting New Testament Criticism.* Minneapolis: Fortress Press, 1995.

Brown, Raymond. *The Death of the Messiah.* New York: Doubleday, 1994.

Charlesworth, J. ed. *The Messiah: Developments in Earliest Judaism and Christianity.* Minneapolis: Fortress Press, 1992.

Dahl, Nils A. *Jesus the Christ.* Minneapolis: Fortress Press, 1991.

Donahue, John. *The Gospel in Parable.* Philadelphia: Fortress Press, 1988.

Gamble, Harry. *Books and Readers in the Early Church: A History of Early Christian Texts.* New Haven: Yale University Press, 1995.

Juel, Donald. *Mark.* Augsburg Commentary on the New Testament Series. Minneapolis: Augsburg Publishing House, 1990.

———. *A Master of Surprise.* Minneapolis: Augsburg Publishing House, 1994.

Kermode, Frank. *Genesis of Secrecy: On the Interpretation of Narrative.* Cambridge, Mass.: Harvard University Press, 1979.

Perrin, Norman. *What Is Redaction Criticism?* Philadelphia: Fortress Press, 1969.

Rhoads, David, and Donald Michie. *Mark as Story.* Philadelphia: Fortress Press, 1982.

Tolbert, Mary Ann. *Sowing the Gospel: Mark's World in Literary-Historical Perspective.* Minneapolis: Fortress Press, 1989.

Williamson, Lamar. *Mark.* Atlanta: John Knox Press, 1983.

Wrede, Wilhelm. *The Messianic Secret.* Trans. J. C. G. Greig. Cambridge: J. Clarke, 1971.

INDEX OF ANCIENT AND MODERN AUTHORS

Aland, Barbara, 197 n. 1
Aland, Kurt, 196 (chap. 6) n. 2, (chap. 9) n. 1
Anselm of Canterbury, 158, 160, 196 (chap. 8) n. 2
Aristotle, 33, 40
Auerbach, Eric, 141-43, 194 n. 23
Augustine of Hippo, 19-20
Austin, J. L., 178

Best, Ernest, 28, 194 n. 13
Brown, Raymond, 153, 195 (chap. 2) n. 3, 196 (chap. 7) n. 2

Charlesworth, James, 154, 195 (chap. 4) n. 2, 196 (chap. 7) n. 3
Chatman, Seymour, 30

Dibelius, Martin, 119, 193 n. 3
Donahue, John, 28, 194 nn. 14, 17

Euripides, 32
Eusebius, 18, 193 n. 1

Fish, Stanley, 29, 194 n. 18
Forde, Gerhard, 196 (chap. 8) n. 1
Fowler, Robert, 29-30, 174, 194 nn. 19, 22, 197 (chap. 9) n. 5, (chap. 10) n. 1

Gamble, Harry, 194 n. 25
Green, W. S., 195 (chap. 4) n. 1
Greer, Rowan, 195 (chap. 4) n. 1
Griesbach, Johann, 19-20
Gros-Louis, Kenneth, 193 n. 8

Hare, Douglas, 194 n. 24
Homer, 142

Jeremias, Joachim, 121-23, 183-84, 196 (chap. 6) nn. 1, 3, 197 (chap. 10) n. 3
Jerome, 168
Josephus, 58, 67, 195 (chap. 1) n. 2
Juel, Donald, 193 n. 2, 194 nn. 11, 14, 24, 195 (chap. 4) n. 1, 196 (chap. 4) n. 3, (chap. 6) n. 5, (chap. 7) n. 1

Kee, Howard Clark, 194 n. 20
Keifert, Patrick, 193 n. 5
Kellogg, Robert, 29
Kermode, Frank, 26, 127-28, 174-75, 183, 190, 193 n. 9, 196 (chap. 6) n. 4, 197 (chap. 9) nn. 2, 6, (chap. 10) n. 4

Kuerzinger, Joseph, 193 n. 2
Kugel, James, 195 (chap. 4) n. 1

Lachmann, Karl, 20
Lewis, C. S., 160-63, 196 (chap. 8)
    nn. 3-6
Lincoln, Andrew, 197 (chap. 9) n. 3
Lindars, Barnabas, 194 n. 24

McGowan, Alec, 48
Marxsen, Willi, 26, 193 n. 7
Matera, Frank, 194 n. 14
Michie, Donald, 28, 194 n. 15
Myers, Ched, 196 (chap. 5) n. 1

Papias, 18-20, 26, 193 nn. 1, 2
Perrin, Norman, 26, 193 n. 10
Petronius, 142

Rhoads, David, 28, 41, 48, 194 n. 15
Ricoeur, Paul, 22
Rivkin, Ellis, 195 (chap. 2) n. 2

Sanders, E. P., 195 (chap. 2) n. 2
Schmidt, Karl, 22, 193 n. 6
Scholes, Robert, 29
Schurer, Emil, 195 (chap. 2) n. 1
Schüssler Fiorenza, Elisabeth, 74,
    195 (chap. 2) n. 4
Schweitzer, Albert, 40-41, 51, 118,
    194 n. 21, 196 (chap. 5) n. 2
Spiegel, Shalom, 195 (chap. 1) n. 4
Sternberg, Meir, 128, 196 (chap. 6)
    n. 5

Tacitus, 142
Tannehill, Robert, 28, 174, 194 n.
    12, 197 (chap. 9) n. 4, (chap.
    10) n. 2
Tolbert, Mary Ann, 28, 194 n. 16

Winter, Paul, 195 (chap. 2) n. 2
Wrede, Wilhelm, 21, 177, 182, 193
    n. 4